# Node.js High Performance

Take your application to the next level of high performance using the extensive capabilities of Node.js

**Diogo Resende**

PACKT PUBLISHING

open source*
community experience distilled

BIRMINGHAM - MUMBAI

# Node.js High Performance

Copyright © 2015 Packt Publishing

All rights reserved. No part of this book may be reproduced, stored in a retrieval system, or transmitted in any form or by any means, without the prior written permission of the publisher, except in the case of brief quotations embedded in critical articles or reviews.

Every effort has been made in the preparation of this book to ensure the accuracy of the information presented. However, the information contained in this book is sold without warranty, either express or implied. Neither the author, nor Packt Publishing, and its dealers and distributors will be held liable for any damages caused or alleged to be caused directly or indirectly by this book.

Packt Publishing has endeavored to provide trademark information about all of the companies and products mentioned in this book by the appropriate use of capitals. However, Packt Publishing cannot guarantee the accuracy of this information.

First published: August 2015

Production reference: 1120815

Published by Packt Publishing Ltd.
Livery Place
35 Livery Street
Birmingham B3 2PB, UK.

ISBN 978-1-78528-614-8

www.packtpub.com

# Credits

**Author**
Diogo Resende

**Reviewers**
Abhishek Dey
Glenn Geenen
Stefan Lapers
Aravind V.S

**Commissioning Editor**
Ashwin Nair

**Acquisition Editor**
Sonali Vernekar

**Content Development Editor**
Rashmi Suvarna

**Technical Editor**
Utkarsha S. Kadam

**Copy Editor**
Vikrant Phadkay

**Project Coordinator**
Judie Jose

**Proofreader**
Safis Editing

**Indexer**
Rekha Nair

**Production Coordinator**
Manu Joseph

**Cover Work**
Manu Joseph

# About the Author

**Diogo Resende** is a passionate developer obsessed with perfection in everything he works on. He loves everything about the Internet of Things, which is the ability to connect everything together and always be connected to the world.

He studied computer science and graduated in engineering. At that time, he deepened his knowledge of computer networking and security, software development, and cloud computing. Over the past 10 years, Diogo has embraced different challenges to develop applications and services to connect people with embedded devices around the world, building a bridge between old and uncommon protocols and the Internet of today.

ThinkDigital has been his employer and a major part of his life for the last few years. It offers services and expertise in areas such as computer networking and security, automation, smart metering, and fleet management and intelligence. Diogo has also published many open source projects. You can find them all, with an MIT license style, on his personal GitHub page under the username dresende.

> First of all, I would like to thank my wife, Ana, for putting up with my late-night writing sessions. She has given me enough of the space and tranquility that I needed to take up this challenge. I would also like to thank my son, Manuel, for being born exactly when I started writing the book, for stealing my attention but also making my days happier, and for giving me the strength to carry on and overcome every obstacle.
>
> Last but not least, I would like to thank everyone in my company for putting up with me. I thank my business associate, Nuno, and my work colleagues Sílvia, Luis, and Helder for collaborating and helping the company go ahead and achieve all our dreams.

# About the Reviewers

**Abhishek Dey** was born in Bandel, West Bengal, India. He holds an MS degree in computer engineering from the University of Florida, Gainesville, USA. His research interests lie primarily in the fields of compiler design, computer security, networks, data mining, analyses of algorithms, and concurrency and parallelism. He is a passionate programmer, who started programming in C and Java at the age of 10. Shortly afterwards, he developed a strong interest in web technologies and system implementation.

Abhishek possesses profound expertise in developing high-volume software using C++, Java, C#, JavaScript, jQuery, AngularJS, and HTML5. He also enjoys coding in functional programming languages, such as SML. Some of his recent projects can be found at `https://github.com/deyabhishek`.

He is a Microsoft Certified Professional, an Oracle Certified Java Programmer, an Oracle Certified Professional Java EE Web Component Developer, and an Oracle Certified Professional Java EE Business Component Developer.

In his leisure time, Abhishek loves to listen to music, travel to interesting places, and paint something on canvas, giving colors to his imagination. More information about him can be found at `http://abhishekdey.com`.

He has reviewed *Kali Linux CTF Blueprints*, *AngularJS UI Development*, *RESTful Web API Design with Node.js*, and *Mastering AngularJS for .NET Developers*, all by Packt Publishing.

**Glenn Geenen** is a Node.js developer with a background in game and mobile development. He worked mostly as an iOS consultant before becoming a Node.js consultant for his own company, GeenenTijd.

**Stefan Lapers** started his career almost 20 years ago as an IT support engineer. Then, he quickly grew in the field of Linux/Unix system engineering and software development.

Over the years, he has gained experience in deploying and maintaining hosted application solutions while working for prominent customers, such as MTV, TMF, and many more. In recent years, Stefan was involved in multiple development projects and their delivery as services on the Internet.

In his spare time, he enjoys being with his family and flying remotely controlled helicopters.

**Aravind V.S** is an aspiring mind and a creative brain to look forward to in the field of technology. He is a successful entrepreneur, developer, and technology consultant whose interest in embedded systems and computers paved his way into the programming world at the age of 15. At that time, he developed a full-fledged stock and inventory management system for a family friend. He has cofounded Entity Business Foundations, a web and mobile technology start-up based in Kerala (`https://teamebf.com/`); founded ioStash, an open source Internet of Things platform (`http://iostash.com/`); and tailored cloud:VAR, an open source backendless web application framework (`http://cloudvar.org/`) written in NodeJS and MongoDB.

In his spare time, Aravind can be found outdoors, focusing his camera, reading books, or writing articles for his blog at `http://aravindvs.com/blog/`. He has previously reviewed *NodeJS Cookbook* and *NodeJS Essentials* by Packt Publishing. Currently, he works as the chief technology officer at Entity Business Foundations. You can contact him at `mail@aravindvs.com`.

> I would like to take this opportunity to thank my friends—Harikrishnan, Abdulla Ahsan, and Muhammed Anas—and my parents for their support in completing the review of this book. Thanks especially to my best friend, Kavya Babu, for her enduring support, encouragement, and faith in me, without which I wouldn't have been what I am today. Above all, I'd like to thank the Almighty for giving me everything I needed at the right time.

# www.PacktPub.com

## Support files, eBooks, discount offers, and more

For support files and downloads related to your book, please visit www.PacktPub.com.

Did you know that Packt offers eBook versions of every book published, with PDF and ePub files available? You can upgrade to the eBook version at www.PacktPub.com and as a print book customer, you are entitled to a discount on the eBook copy. Get in touch with us at service@packtpub.com for more details.

At www.PacktPub.com, you can also read a collection of free technical articles, sign up for a range of free newsletters and receive exclusive discounts and offers on Packt books and eBooks.

![PacktLib]

https://www2.packtpub.com/books/subscription/packtlib

Do you need instant solutions to your IT questions? PacktLib is Packt's online digital book library. Here, you can search, access, and read Packt's entire library of books.

### Why subscribe?

- Fully searchable across every book published by Packt
- Copy and paste, print, and bookmark content
- On demand and accessible via a web browser

### Free access for Packt account holders

If you have an account with Packt at www.PacktPub.com, you can use this to access PacktLib today and view 9 entirely free books. Simply use your login credentials for immediate access.

# Table of Contents

| | |
|---|---|
| **Preface** | **v** |
| **Chapter 1: Introduction and Composition** | **1** |
|   **Performance analysis** | **2** |
|     Monitoring | 3 |
|   **Getting high performance** | **4** |
|     Testing and benchmarking | 5 |
|     Composition in applications | 6 |
|       Using NPM | 7 |
|       Separating your code | 7 |
|       Embracing asynchronous tasks | 8 |
|       Using library functions | 9 |
|       Using function rules | 9 |
|       Testing your modules | 10 |
|   **Summary** | **11** |
| **Chapter 2: Development Patterns** | **13** |
|   **What are patterns?** | **13** |
|   **Node.js patterns** | **15** |
|   **Types of patterns** | **16** |
|     Architectural patterns | 16 |
|     Creational patterns | 21 |
|     Structural patterns | 23 |
|     Behavioral patterns | 25 |
|   **Event-driven architecture** | **27** |
|     Streams | 28 |
|     Buffers | 29 |
|   **Optimizations** | **29** |
|     Hidden types | 30 |
|     Numbers | 30 |
|     Arrays | 31 |

| | |
|---|---|
| Functions | 31 |
| The for-in loops | 32 |
| The infinite loops | 32 |
| The try-catch blocks | 32 |
| Eval | 32 |
| **Summary** | **33** |
| **Chapter 3: Garbage Collection** | **35** |
| **Automatic memory management** | **35** |
| Memory organization | 37 |
| Memory leaks | 38 |
| Event emitters | 39 |
| Referencing objects | 40 |
| Object representation | 42 |
| Object heaps | 42 |
| Heap snapshots | 43 |
| Third-party management | 54 |
| **Summary** | **54** |
| **Chapter 4: CPU Profiling** | **55** |
| **The I/O library** | **56** |
| Fibonacci | 57 |
| Flame graphs | 62 |
| Profiling alternatives | 68 |
| **Summary** | **68** |
| **Chapter 5: Data and Cache** | **71** |
| **Data storage** | **72** |
| Excessive I/O | 72 |
| **Database management systems** | **73** |
| Caching data | 74 |
| Asynchronous caching | 75 |
| Clustering data | 78 |
| Accessing data | 80 |
| **Summary** | **81** |
| **Chapter 6: Test, Benchmark, and Analyze** | **83** |
| **Test fundamentals** | **84** |
| The test environment | 85 |
| The Docker tool | 85 |
| The test tool | 87 |
| Continuous integration | 92 |
| Code coverage | 93 |

| | |
|---|---|
| Benchmark tests | 96 |
| Analyzing tests | 98 |
| **Summary** | **99** |
| **Chapter 7: Bottlenecks** | **101** |
| **Host limits** | **102** |
| Network limits | 104 |
| Client limits | 107 |
| Browser limits | 108 |
| Performance variables | 110 |
| **Summary** | **110** |
| **Index** | **111** |

# Preface

High performance on a platform such as Node.js means knowing how to take advantage of every aspect of your hardware and helping memory management act at its best and correctly decide how to architect a complex application. Do not panic if your application starts consuming a lot of memory. Instead, spot the leak and solve it fast. Better yet, monitor and stop it before it becomes an issue.

## What this book covers

*Chapter 1*, *Introduction and Composition*, introduces the subject, emphasizing performance analysis and the importance of benchmarking. It's about splitting applications into several smaller components, reducing the complexity of each component to a manageable level for the developers involved in the application. Here, you understand the importance of developing methodologies to break complexity into smaller and reusable modules that can more easily be analyzed and exchanged with other new and better modules during the course of the application's life cycle.

*Chapter 2*, *Development Patterns*, is about good programming patterns that help avoid performance penalties or help find them. You'll value the importance of carefully choosing techniques and patterns that are simple, and avoid future problems. With this in mind, you'll better understand how the language works, the importance of knowing the event loop, how asynchronous programming works best, and some of the first-class citizens of the language—streams and buffers.

*Chapter 3*, *Garbage Collection*, covers GC, its importance, and its behavior. Here, you get to understand V8 memory management, dead memory, and memory leaks. You also learn how to profile an application and spot memory leaks caused by bad programming where a developer hasn't deferenced objects correctly.

*Chapter 4*, *CPU Profiling*, is about profiling the processor and understanding when and why your application hogs your host. In this chapter, you understand the limits of the language and how to develop applications that can be divided into several components running across different hosts, allowing better performance and scalability.

*Chapter 5*, *Data and Cache*, explains externally stored application data and how it can affect your application's performance. It's about data stored locally in the application, the disk, a local service, a local network service or even the client host. In this chapter, you get to know that different types of data storage methods have different penalties, and these must be considered when choosing the best one. You learn that data can be stored locally or remotely and access to the data can be — and should be — cached sometimes, depending on the importance of the data.

*Chapter 6*, *Test, Benchmark, and Analyze*, is about testing and benchmarking applications. It's also about enforcing code coverage to avoid unknown application test zones. Then we cover benchmarks and benchmark analytics. You get to understand how good tests can pinpoint where to benchmark and analyze specific parts of the application to allow performance improvements.

*Chapter 7*, *Bottlenecks*, covers limits outside the application. This chapter is about the situations when you realize that the performance limit is not because of the application programing but external factors, such as the host hardware, network or client. You'll become aware of the limits that external components can impose on the application, locally or remotely. Moreover, the chapter explains that sometimes, the limits are on the client side and nothing can be done to improve the current performance.

# What you need for this book

The only software needed is Node.js. Some modules might need compilation, so a Linux or OS X operating system is easier for testing of the examples. No specific hardware is needed.

# Who this book is for

The book is intended for those with a basic Node.js background and those in need of a more in-depth understanding of this platform. Maybe, you're comfortable with the language and perhaps you know that it has a garbage collector, but you never really understand how it works and how it fails to work depending on the way you use the language. Basic language understanding and solid experience are required.

# Conventions

In this book, you will find a number of text styles that distinguish between different kinds of information. Here are some examples of these styles and an explanation of their meaning.

Code words in text, database table names, folder names, filenames, file extensions, pathnames, dummy URLs, user input, and Twitter handles are shown as follows: "We can include other contexts through the use of the `include` directive."

A block of code is set as follows:

```
async.each(users, function (user, next) {
    // do something on each user object
    return next();
}, function (err) {
    // done!
});
```

Any command-line input or output is written as follows:

```
$ node --debug leaky.js
Debugger listening on port 5858
mem. nodes: 37293
mem. nodes: 37645
mem. nodes: 37951
mem. nodes: 37991
mem. nodes: 38004
```

**New terms** and **important words** are shown in bold. Words that you see on the screen, for example, in menus or dialog boxes, appear in the text like this: "Now, instead of choosing **Take Snapshot**, just click on the **Load** button and choose the snapshots from your disk."

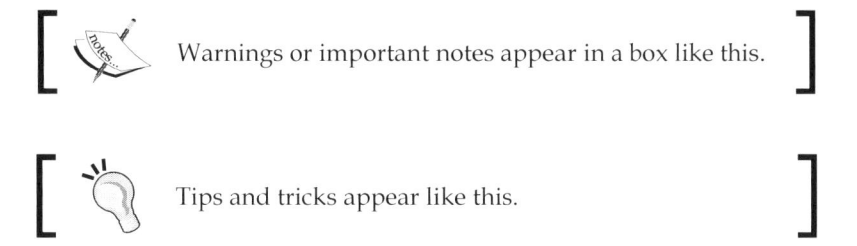

> Warnings or important notes appear in a box like this.

> Tips and tricks appear like this.

# Reader feedback

Feedback from our readers is always welcome. Let us know what you think about this book—what you liked or disliked. Reader feedback is important for us as it helps us develop titles that you will really get the most out of.

To send us general feedback, simply e-mail feedback@packtpub.com, and mention the book's title in the subject of your message.

If there is a topic that you have expertise in and you are interested in either writing or contributing to a book, see our author guide at www.packtpub.com/authors.

# Customer support

Now that you are the proud owner of a Packt book, we have a number of things to help you to get the most from your purchase.

## Downloading the example code

You can download the example code files from your account at http://www.packtpub.com for all the Packt Publishing books you have purchased. If you purchased this book elsewhere, you can visit http://www.packtpub.com/support and register to have the files e-mailed directly to you.

## Downloading the color images of this book

We also provide you with a PDF file that has color images of the screenshots/diagrams used in this book. The color images will help you better understand the changes in the output. You can download this file from https://www.packtpub.com/sites/default/files/downloads/6148OS.pdf.

## Errata

Although we have taken every care to ensure the accuracy of our content, mistakes do happen. If you find a mistake in one of our books—maybe a mistake in the text or the code—we would be grateful if you could report this to us. By doing so, you can save other readers from frustration and help us improve subsequent versions of this book. If you find any errata, please report them by visiting http://www.packtpub.com/submit-errata, selecting your book, clicking on the **Errata Submission Form** link, and entering the details of your errata. Once your errata are verified, your submission will be accepted and the errata will be uploaded to our website or added to any list of existing errata under the Errata section of that title.

To view the previously submitted errata, go to `https://www.packtpub.com/books/content/support` and enter the name of the book in the search field. The required information will appear under the **Errata** section.

# Piracy

Piracy of copyrighted material on the Internet is an ongoing problem across all media. At Packt, we take the protection of our copyright and licenses very seriously. If you come across any illegal copies of our works in any form on the Internet, please provide us with the location address or website name immediately so that we can pursue a remedy.

Please contact us at `copyright@packtpub.com` with a link to the suspected pirated material.

We appreciate your help in protecting our authors and our ability to bring you valuable content.

# Questions

If you have a problem with any aspect of this book, you can contact us at `questions@packtpub.com`, and we will do our best to address the problem.

# Introduction and Composition

High performance is hard, and it depends on many factors. Best performance should be a constant goal for developers. To achieve it, a developer must know the programming language they use and, more importantly, how the language performs under heavy loads, these being disk, memory, network, and processor usage.

Developers will make the most out of a language if they know its weaknesses. In a perfect world, since every job is different, a developer should look for the best tool for the job. But this is not feasible and a developer wouldn't be able to know every best tool, so they have to look for the second best tool for every job. A developer will excel if they know few tools but master them.

As a metaphor, a hammer is used to drive nails, and you can also use it to break objects apart or forge metals, but you shouldn't use it to drive screws. The same applies to languages and platforms. Some platforms are very good for a lot of jobs but perform really badly at other jobs. This performance can sometimes be mitigated, but at other times, can't be avoided and you should look for better tools.

Node.js is not a language; it's actually a platform built on top of V8, Google's open source JavaScript engine. This engine implements ECMAScript, which itself is a simple and very flexible language. I say "simple" because it has no way of accessing the network, accessing the disk, or talking to other processes. It can't even stop execution since it has no kind of exit instruction. This language needs some kind of interface model on top of it to be useful. Node.js does this by exposing a (preferably) nonblocking I/O model using libuv. This nonblocking API allows you to access the filesystem, connect to network services and execute child processes.

The API also has two other important elements: buffers and streams. Since JavaScript strings are Unicode friendly, buffers were introduced to help deal with binary data. Streams are used as simple event interfaces to pass data around. Buffers and streams are used all over the API when reading file contents or receiving network packets.

A stream is a module, similar to the network module. When loaded, it provides access to some base classes that help create readable, writable, duplex, and transform streams. These can be used to perform all sorts of data manipulation in a simplified and unified format.

The buffers module easily becomes your best friend when converting binary data formats to some other format, for example, JSON. Multiple read and write methods help you convert integers and floats, signed or not, big endian or little endian, from 8 bits to 8 bytes long.

Most of the platform is designed to be simple, small, and stable. It's designed and ready to create some high-performance applications.

# Performance analysis

Performance is the amount of work completed in a defined period of time and with a set of defined resources. It can be analyzed using one or more metrics that depend on the performance goal. The goal can be low latency, low memory footprint, reduced processor usage, or even reduced power consumption.

The act of performance analysis is also called **profiling**. Profiling is very important for making optimized applications and is achieved by instrumenting either the source or the instance of the application. By instrumenting the source, developers can spot common performance weak spots. By instrumenting an application instance, they can test the application on different environments. This type of instrumentation can also be known by the name **benchmarking**.

Node.js is known for being fast. Actually, it's not that fast; it's just as fast as your resources allow it. What Node.js is best at is not blocking your application because of an I/O task. The perception of performance can be misleading in Node.js applications. In some other languages, when an application task gets blocked—for example, by a disk operation—all other tasks can be affected. In the case of Node.js, this doesn't happen—usually.

Some people look at the platform as being single threaded, which isn't true. Your code runs on a thread, but there are a few more threads responsible for I/O operations. Since these operations are extremely slow compared to the processor's performance, they run on a separate thread and signal the platform when they have information for your application. Applications blocking I/O operations perform poorly. Since Node.js doesn't block I/O unless you want it to, other operations can be performed while waiting for I/O. This greatly improves performance.

V8 is an open source Google project and is the JavaScript engine behind Node.js. It's responsible for compiling and executing JavaScript, as well as managing your application's memory needs. It is designed with performance in mind. V8 follows several design principles to improve language performance. The engine has a profiler and one of the best and fast garbage collectors that exist, which is one of the keys to its performance. It also does not compile the language into byte code; it compiles it directly into machine code on the first execution.

A good background in the development environment will greatly increase the chances of success in developing high-performance applications. It's very important to know how dereferencing works, or why your variables should avoid switching types. Here are other useful tips you would want to follow. You can use a style guide like JSCS and a linter like JSHint to enforce them to for yourself and your team. Here are some of them:

- Write small functions, as they're more easily optimized
- Use monomorphic parameters and variables
- Prefer arrays to manipulate data, as integer-indexed elements are faster
- Try to have small objects and avoid long prototype chains
- Avoid cloning objects beacause big objects will slow the operations

## Monitoring

After an application is put into production mode, performance analysis becomes even more important, as users will be more demanding than you were. Users don't accept anything that takes more than a second, and monitoring the application's behavior over time and over some specific loads will be extremely important, as it will point to you where your platform is failing or will fail next.

Yes, your application may fail, and the best you can do is be prepared. Create a backup plan, have fallback hardware, and create service probes. Essentially, anticipate all the scenarios you can think of, and remember that your application will still fail. Here are some of those scenarios and aspects that you should monitor:

- When in production, application usage is of extreme importance to understand where your application is heading in terms of data size or memory usage. It's important that you carefully define source code probes to monitor metrics — not only performance metrics, such as requests per second or concurrent requests, but also error rate and exception percentage per request served. Your application emits errors and sometimes throws exceptions; it's normal and you shouldn't ignore them.

- Don't forget the rest of the infrastructure. If your application must perform at high standards, your infrastructure should too. Your server power supply should be uninterruptible and stable, as instability will degrade your hardware faster than it should.

- Choose your disks wisely, as faster disks are more expensive and usually come in smaller storage sizes. Sometimes, however, this is actually not a bad decision when your application doesn't need that much storage and speed is considered more important. But don't just look at the gigabytes per dollar. Sometimes, it's more important to look at the gigabits per second per dollar.

- Also, your server temperature and server room should be monitored. High temperatures degrades performance and your hardware has an operation temperature limit. Security, both physical and virtual, is also very important. Everything counts for the standards of high performance, as an application that stops serving its users is not performing at all.

# Getting high performance

Planning is essential in order to achieve the best results possible. High performance is built from the ground up and starts with how you plan and develop. It obviously depends on physical resources, as you can't perform well when you don't have sufficient memory to accomplish your task, but it also depends greatly on how you plan and develop an application. Mastering tools will give much better performance chances than just using them.

Setting the bar high from the beginning of development will force the planning to be more prudent. Some bad planning of the database layer can really downgrade performance. Also, cautious planning will cause developers to think more about use cases and program more consciously.

High performance is when you have to think about a new set of resources (processor, memory, storage) because all that you have is exhausted, not just because one resource is. A high-performance application shouldn't need a second server when a little processor is used and the disk is full. In such a case, you just need bigger disks.

Applications can't be designed as monolithic these days. An increasing user base enforces a distributed architecture, or at least one that can distribute load by having multiple instances. This is very important to accommodate in the beginning of the planning, as it will be harder to change an application that is already in production.

*Chapter 1*

Most common applications will start performing worse over time, not because of deficit of processing power but because of increasing data size on databases and disks. You'll notice that the importance of memory increases and fallback disks become critical to avoiding downtime. It's very important that an application be able to scale horizontally, whether to shard data across servers or across regions.

A distributed architecture also increases performance. Geographically distributed servers can be more closed to clients and give a perception of performance. Also, databases distributed by more servers will handle more traffic as a whole and allow DevOps to accomplish zero downtime goals. This is also very useful for maintenance, as nodes can be brought down for support without affecting the application.

# Testing and benchmarking

To know whether an application performs well or not under specific environments, we have to test it. This kind of test is called a benchmark. Benchmarking is important to do and it's specific to every application. Even for the same language and platform, different applications might perform differently, either because of the way in which some parts of an application were structured or the way in which a database was designed.

Analyzing the performance will indicate bottleneck of your application, or if you may, the parts of the application that perform not good as others. These are the parts that need to be improved. Constantly trying to improve the worst performing parts will elevate the application's overall performance.

There are plenty of tools out there, some more specific or focused on JavaScript applications, such as benchmarkjs (http://benchmarkjs.com/) and ben (https://github.com/substack/node-ben), and others more generic, such as ab (http://httpd.apache.org/docs/2.2/programs/ab.html) and httpload (https://github.com/perusio/httpload). There are several types of benchmark tests depending on the goal, they are as follows:

- **Load testing** is the simplest form of benchmarking. It is done to find out how the application performs under a specific load. You can test and find out how many connections an application accepts per second, or how many traffic bytes an application can handle. An application load can be checked by looking at the external performance, such as traffic, and also internal performance, such as the processor used or the memory consumed.

- **Soak testing** is used to see how an application performs during a more extended period of time. It is done when an application tends to degrade over time and analysis is needed to see how it reacts. This type of test is important in order to detect memory leaks, as some applications can perform well in some basic tests, but over time, the memory leaks and their performance can degrade.

- **Spike testing** is used when a load is increased very fast to see how the application reacts and performs. This test is very useful and important in applications that can have spike usages, and operators need to know how the application will react. Twitter is a good example of an application environment that can be affected by usage spikes (in world events such as sports or religious dates), and need to know how the infrastructure will handle them.

All of these tests can become harder as your application grows. Since your user base gets bigger, your application scales and you lose the ability to be able to load test with the resources you have. It's good to be prepared for this moment, especially to be prepared to monitor performance and keep track of soaks and spikes as your application users start to be the ones responsible for continuously test load.

# Composition in applications

Because of this continuous demand of performant applications, composition becomes very important. Composition is a practice where you split the application into several smaller and simpler parts, making them easier to understand, develop, and maintain. It also makes them easier to test and improve.

Avoid creating big, monolithic code bases. They don't work well when you need to make a change, and they also don't work well if you need to test and analyze any part of the code to improve it and make it perform better.

The Node.js platform helps you—and in some ways, forces you to—compose your code. **Node.js Package Manager** (**NPM**) is a great module publishing service. You can download other people's modules and publish your own as well. There are tens of thousands of modules published, which means that you don't have to reinvent the wheel in most cases. This is good since you can avoid wasting time on creating a module and use a module that is already in production and used by many people, which normally means that bugs will be tracked faster and improvements will be delivered even faster.

The Node.js platform allows developers to easily separate code. You don't have to do this, as the platform doesn't force you to, but you should try and follow some good practices, such as the ones described in the following sections.

## Using NPM

Don't rewrite code unless you need to. Take your time to try some available modules, and choose the one that is right for you. This reduces the probability of writing faulty code and helps published modules that have a bigger user base. Bugs will be spotted earlier, and more people in different environments will test fixes. Moreover, you will be using a more resilient module.

One important and neglected task after starting to use some modules is to track changes and, whenever possible, keep using recent stable versions. If a dependency module has not been updated for a year, you can spot a problem later, but you will have a hard time figuring out what changed between two versions that are a year apart. Node.js modules tend to be improved over time and API changes are not rare. Always upgrade with caution and don't forget to test.

## Separating your code

Again, you should always split your code into smaller parts. Node.js helps you do this in a very easy way. You should not have files bigger than 5 kB. If you have, you better think about splitting it. Also, as a good rule, each user-defined object should have its own separate file. Name your files accordingly:

```
// MyObject.js
module.exports = MyObject;

function MyObject() {
  // ...
}
MyObject.prototype.myMethod = function () { ... };
```

Another good rule to check whether you have a file bigger than it should be; that is, it should be easy to read and understand in less than 5 minutes by someone new to the application. If not, it means that it's too complex and it will be harder to track and fix bugs later on.

> Remember that later on, when your application becomes huge, you will be like a new developer when opening a file to fix something. You can't remember all of the code of the application, and you need to absorb a file behavior fast.

## Embracing asynchronous tasks

The platform is designed to be asynchronous, so you shouldn't go against it. Sometimes, it can be really hard to make some recursive tasks or even simply cycle through a list of tasks that have to run serially. You should avoid creating a module to handle asynchronous tasks, as there are some used and tested by hundreds of thousands of people out there. For instance, async is a simple and very practical way of helping the developer perform better, and the learning curve is very smooth:

```
async.each(users, function (user, next) {
    // do something on each user object
    return next();
}, function (err) {
    // done!
});
```

This module has a lot of methods similar to the ones you find in the array object, such as map, reduce, filter, and each, but for iterating asynchronously. This is extremely useful when your application gets more complex and some user actions require some serialized tasks. Error handling is also done correctly and the execution stop is done as expected. The module helps run serial or parallel tasks.

Also, serial tasks that would usually enforce a developer to nest calls and enter the callback hell can simply be avoided. This is especially useful when, for example, you need to perform a transaction on a database with several queries involved.

Another common mistake when writing asynchronous code is throwing errors. Callbacks are called outside the scope where they are defined, and so you cannot just put the callback inside a try/catch block. Therefore, avoid doing this unless it's a very critical error that should make your application stop and quit. In Node.js, throwing an exception without catching it will trigger an uncaughtException event.

The platform has a rule that is consensual for most developers—the so-called error-first callback style. This rule is of extreme importance, since it allows an easier reuse of your code. Even if you have a function where there's no chance of throwing an error, or when you just don't want it to throw and use some kind of error handling inside the function, your callback should always reserve the first argument for an error event if it's always null. This will allow your function to be used with an async module. Also, other developers will be counting on this style when debugging, so always reverse the first argument as an error object.

Plus, you should always reserve the last argument of the function as the callback. Never define arguments after your callback:

```
function mySuperFunction(arg1, ..., argN, next) {
    // do some voodoo
```

```
        return next(null, my_result); // 1st argument reserved for
          error
}
```

## Using library functions

Library functions are another type of module you should use. They help in handling repetitive tasks, and every developer has to perform such tasks. Some of these repetitive tasks can be done with no effort, just by using a library function from lodash or underscore. They are an important part of your code and have good optimizations that you don't even have to think about. Many cycling tasks, such as finding an object in an array based on an object key, or mapping an array of objects to an array of keys of every object, are one-liners in these libraries. Read the documentation first to avoid using the library and not fully using its potential.

Although these kinds of modules can be useful, they can also downgrade performance if they are not chosen well. Some modules are designed to help developers in some tasks, but do not target performance—just convenience. In other words, these modules can help you develop faster, but you shouldn't forget the complexity of each function. Otherwise, you will be calling the same function several times because you forget about its complexity, instead of calling it once and saving the results.

> Remember that high performance is not seen when you develop the application and test with one or two users. At that time, the application performs at a good speed, since data size and user count is still small. It's later on that you may regret some of your design decisions.

## Using function rules

Functions are very important in this platform. This is no surprise since the language is functional and has first-class functions. There are some rules you should follow when writing functions that will make your life easier when debugging or optimizing it later. They also avoid some errors as they try to enforce some common structure. Once again, you can enforce these rules using, for example, JSCS (http://jscs.info/):

1. Always name your functions, especially when they're closures used as callbacks. This allows you to identify them in stack traces when your code breaks. Also, they allow a new developer to rapidly know what the function is supposed to do. Still, avoid long names:

   ```
   socket.on("data", function onSocketData(data) {
   
       // ...
   
   });
   ```

2. Don't nest your conditions, and return as early as possible. If you have a condition that must return something in a function and if you return, you don't have to use the `else` statement. You also avoid a new indent level, reducing your code and simplifying its revision. If you don't do this, you will end up in a condition hell, with several levels if you have two or more conditions to satisfy:

   ```
   // do this
   if (someCondition) {
       return false;
   }
   return someThing;

   // instead of this:
   if (someCondition) {
       return false;
   } else {
       return someThing;
   }
   ```

3. Create small and simple functions. Don't span your functions for more lines than your screen can handle. Even if your task cannot be reused, split the function into smaller ones. It is even better to put it into a new module and publish it. In this way, you can reuse them at the frontend if you need them. This can also allow the engine to optimize some smaller functions when it is unable to optimize the previous big function. Again, this is important if you don't want a developer to be reading your application code for a week or two before being able to touch anything.

## Testing your modules

Testing your modules is a hard job and is usually neglected, but it's very important to make tests for your modules. The first ones are the hard ones. Look for a test tool that you like, such as vows, chai, or mocha. If you don't know how to start, read a module's documentation, or another module's test code. But don't give up on testing.

> If you need help, read the test tools' websites mentioned earlier, as they usually help you get started. Alternatively, you can take a look at Igor's post (`https://semaphoreci.com/community/tutorials/getting-started-with-node-js-and-mocha`) at semaphore.

After you start adding one or two tests, more will follow. One big advantage of testing your module from the beginning is that when you spot a bug, you can make a test case for it, to be able to reproduce it and avoid it in the future.

Code coverage is not crucial but can help you see how your tests cover your module code base, and if you're just testing a small part. There are some coverage modules, such as `istanbul` or `jscoverage`; choose the one that works best for you. Code coverage is done together with testing, so if you don't test it, you won't be able to see the coverage.

As you might want to improve the performance of an application, every dependency module should be looked at for improvements. This can be done only if you test them. Dependency version management is of great importance, and it can be hard to keep track of new versions and changes, but they might give you some good news. Sometimes, modules are refactored and performance is boosted. A good example of this is database access modules.

# Summary

Together, Node.js and NPM make a very good platform for developing high-performance applications. Since the language behind them is JavaScript and most applications these days are web applications, these combinations make it an even more appealing choice, as it's one less server-side language to learn (such as PHP or Ruby) and can ultimately allow a developer to share code on the client and server sides. Also, frontend and backend developers can share, read, and improve each other's code. Many developers pick this formula and bring with them many of their habits from the client side. Some of these habits are not applicable because on the server side, asynchronous tasks must rule as there are many clients connected (as opposed to one) and performance becomes crucial.

In the next chapter, we will cover some development patterns that help applications stay simple, fast, and scalable as more clients come along and start putting pressure on your infrastructure.

# 2
# Development Patterns

Developing is just great. It gives you a sense of freedom to create new things. This is true for almost every language—a freedom to create something in your own way. This means that there are good ways and not-so-good ways to do the same task. A developer, during the course of their life, will face different problems with similar solutions and will adopt patterns. For some problems, they will know the patterns they are using; for others, they will be using patterns that they probably don't even know.

Some patterns directly increase performance, and others do it indirectly because of an architecture pattern that is able to scale. Creating high-performance applications involves knowing every bit of running code, which results in knowing the patterns used across an application. Sometimes, they're unintentional. At other times, they are enforced because of the benefits of a specific pattern. Patterns are everywhere, from the creation of objects to the interaction between objects and first-class services of an application.

Similarly, there are patterns specific to languages and platforms. This is because the compiler or interpreter handles some pieces of code better than others. Sometimes, it is because it's designed and targeted for best performance on the most common scenarios. At other times, it's just because of how the language treats some entities, such as functions, types of variables, or some loops. Because of all this, knowing how the interpreter treats some code patterns is important.

## What are patterns?

Patterns are not libraries or classes. They're concepts—reusable solutions to common programming problems, tested and optimized for specific use cases. As they're just concepts meant to solve specific problems, they have to be implemented in your language. Every pattern has its advantages and disadvantages, and choosing a wrong pattern for a problem can cause you a big headache.

Patterns can speed up the development process because they provide well-tested and well-proven development paradigms. Reusing patterns helps prevent issues and improves code readability between developers who are familiar with them.

Patterns have a lot of importance in high-performance applications. Sometimes, in order to achieve some flexibility, patterns introduce a new level of indirection in the code, which may reduce performance. You should choose when to introduce a pattern and know when that introduction will hurt the performance metric that you're targeting.

Knowing good patterns is essential in order to avoid the opposite—anti-patterns. An anti-pattern is a solution to a recurring problem that is both ineffective and counterproductive. Anti-patterns are not specific patterns but more like common errors. They are seen by the majority of mature developers/community as strategies that you shouldn't use. Some of the most common and frequent anti-patterns seen are as follows:

- **Repeating yourself**: Don't repeat excessive parts of the code. Lean back, look at the big picture, and refactor it. Some developers tend to look at this refactoring as a complexity of the application, but it can actually make your application simpler. If you think you won't be able to understand the simplicity of your refactoring, don't forget to add a couple of introductory comments to the code.

- **Golden hammer or silver bullet**: Specifically in the Node.js ecosystem, and thanks to NPM, there are literally thousands of modules available out there. Don't reinvent the wheel. Invest your time in using the most common modules for your needs, and avoid recreating them.

- **Coding by exception**: Your code should handle all types of common errors. If the application is well planned, this accidental complexity should be avoided, as it won't bring anything new to the application. Avoid coding for every type of error, handle the most common ones, and default to the most general error. This does not mean that you shouldn't record the error in your backend. Do this so that you can analyze it later, but avoid handling all types of errors. This decreases your code maintenance.

- **Programming by accident**: Don't program by trial and error. Success in this method is pure luck and a question of odds. This is something you should really avoid. Programming by accident can make your code work in some cases, but have erroneous behavior in unplanned situations.

# Node.js patterns

Because of the structure and API model of the Node.js platform, some patterns are more biased or natural. The most obvious are the event-driven and the event stream patterns. They're not enforced but strongly engrained in the core API, and you're forced to use it in some parts of your application, so it's better to know how they work individually, how they work together, and how you can benefit from them.

Using the core API, you can access the filesystem, for example, to read a file with a single method and a callback; or you can request a read stream and then check the data and end events or pipe the stream to somewhere else. This is very useful when, say, you don't want to look at the file and just want to serve it to a client. This architecture was designed to work for core modules such as `http` and `net`. Similarly, when listening for client connections, you'll have to listen for a connection event (unless you have defined a connection listener during socket creation) and then listen for data and end events for each connection. Remember not to ignore error events as they trigger exceptions if not listened and will force your application to stop. Events are the core feature of the Node.js platform:

- Streams are also present, and one might think they're two distinct things, but they're not. Every stream is an extension of an event emitter. In the most basic form, a stream is a process of emitting data events with content from some kind of buffer. Events, streams, and buffers together make a very good example of an event-driven architecture—a pattern that goes very well with the JavaScript language.

- Streams of different types might be connected to each other, especially when sharing common data and end events. It's very common to use an `fs` stream and pipe it to an `http` stream. This usability enables the developer to avoid unnecessary memory allocations in the application and just pass the task to the platform.

- Events enable a loose coupling between application components, enabling it to change and evolve without a strict connection between the components emitting events and the ones listening to them. As a downside, there are some edge cases to look out for, such as losing an emitted event because we were not listening, or leaking memory because of forgetting to stop listening for events that no longer exist.

- Buffers are objects that you should use when manipulating data that might get broken with strings because of the string encoding. They're used by the platform to read files and write data to sockets. Many string manipulation functions are available for buffers to use.

# Types of patterns

Your application won't be using only the core API. In a complex application, you will be using a lot of other modules, some made by you and others that you simply downloaded. Patterns exist everywhere in your application. When you use a module and you need to create a different interface, you would be using the adapter pattern, a structural pattern. If you need to extend the module you just downloaded with a couple of functionality methods, you can use the decorator pattern, another structural pattern. When the downloaded module might need some complex information to initialize, you may want to use the Factory pattern, a creational pattern. If your application evolves and this initialization needs more flexibility, you'll be using the Builder pattern, another creational pattern. If your application accesses relational data, you might have to use the Active Record pattern. If you use some kind of software framework, you might be using the MVC pattern.

Many developers don't notice that they're using some of these patterns. It's important to know them and especially to know the problems that some patterns have in some contexts. In order to be able to analyze and test these patterns, they're categorized into several types. Let's see some of these types and some of the most common patterns for every type.

# Architectural patterns

An architectural pattern is the pattern that is usually implemented inside software frameworks. These solve common problems found across most applications. They avoid code duplication by creating some kind of layer to common broader problems. This image is a description of the Front Controller:

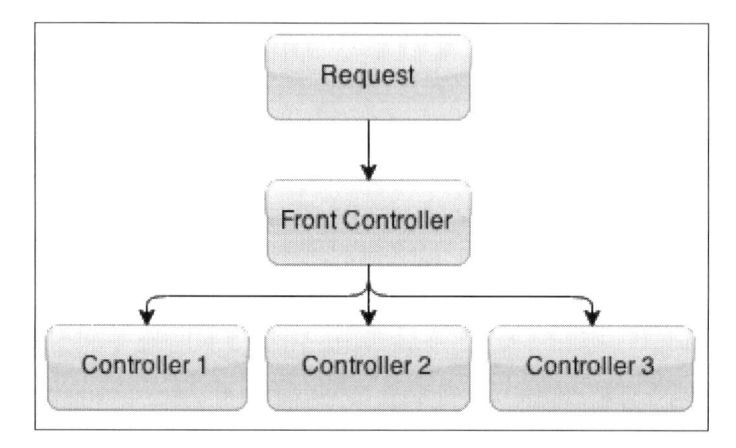

*Chapter 2*

- The **Front Controller** pattern, most commonly seen in web applications, is the case where a unique controller handles all incoming requests. This is achieved by having a single entry point that loads common libraries, such as data access and session management, and then loads the specific controller for each request. This is a very common practice, as the alternative—having several entry points for different actions—would substantially increase and duplicate code, making the application more complex to manage and maintain.

   Present in most frameworks, this pattern allows your application to grow with different modules without duplicating unnecessary code. It has a central point that can handle many common tasks, such as database access, session management, access logging and error logging, generic access, authorization and accounting, and so on.

   This pattern is essential in any well-structured application, as it substantially reduces repeated code by forcing a common part of your application to run first and perform every check that you need. It can also increase security; if you find any breach, it's easier to seal a single entry point than multiple entry points. Using a central point where your application can use all kinds of performance methods to give a better feeling of a responsive application also increases overall performance. The following image is a description of the MVC

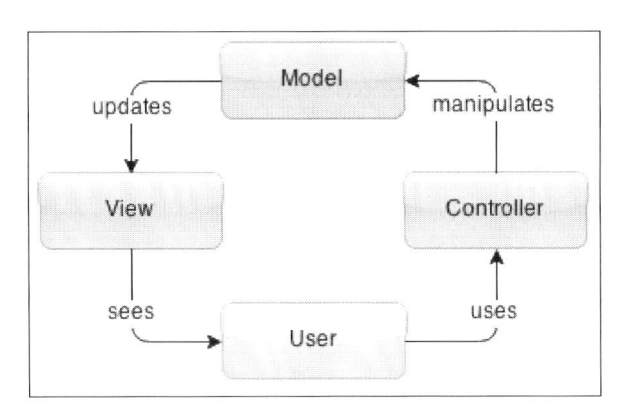

   ![MVC diagram showing Model, View, Controller, and User with relationships: Model updates View, View sees User, User uses Controller, Controller manipulates Model]

- The **Model-View-Controller** (**MVC**) pattern is a pattern that divides an application component into three parts: a model, a view, and a controller (hence the name). The model is your data structure, or your information logic. This can be, for example, one or more tables in a relational database. The view is a visual representation, usually the user interface. It can be graphical or text-based. It's a representation of your model in a way that the user can see and manipulate. The controller is the part responsible for actually manipulating your model—sometimes directly updating the view—as per the actions in the view made by the user.

There are many variations of this pattern and you should choose the one that fits your task and language best. Some of these variations are **Model-View-ViewModel (MVVM)** and **Model-View-Adapter (MVA)**, which try to decouple the view from the model, causing the model to be not necessarily aware of the view. This makes it possible to have several views of the same model.

The main purpose of this pattern is to clearly separate what the user sees (the view, or the design) from the programming logic (the model). This is important in order for designers to be able to change the view without affecting the logic. Also, developers can fix the logic without breaking the design. This pattern is essential if you consider yourself at least an intermediate developer. This is because, more than a pattern, it is considered an essential practice.

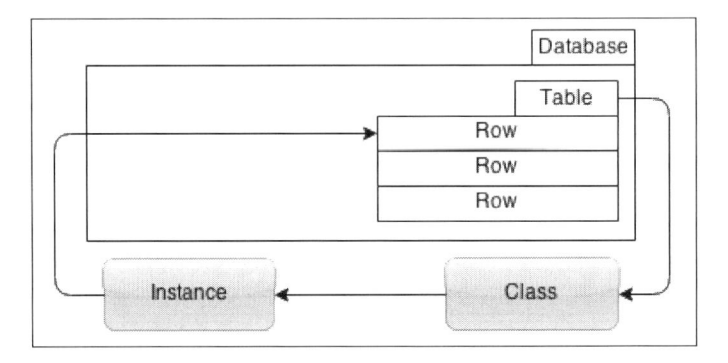

- The **Active Record** pattern is an abstraction layer used to access relational databases by providing a simple data object. Manipulating this object can trigger changes in the database without the developer needing to know what type of database is behind the application. Normally, a table or view in the database is mapped to a class, and instances are mapped to rows. Usually, foreign keys are handled by referencing instances. Logic can be given to the data objects for common application tasks, for example, to calculate a full name based on two different table columns, such as the first name and last name. This, altogether, gives a better approach to the business logic, making it possible to have your data as well as an extra layer on the top extending it to match the projected behavior of the application. The pattern is normally used in **object-relational mapping (ORM)** libraries that extend the functionalities to new levels. An example of this is the possibility to have two or more different places of your application referencing the same row in the database and (without knowing) having the same referenced data object.

This pattern is criticized mainly because of two aspects. The first is that there is an abstraction layer between application and data, which can decrease performance substantially and improve memory leaks in data-intensive applications. Another aspect is the testability; the tight coupling between the data object and database makes it difficult to have a real database for proper testing.

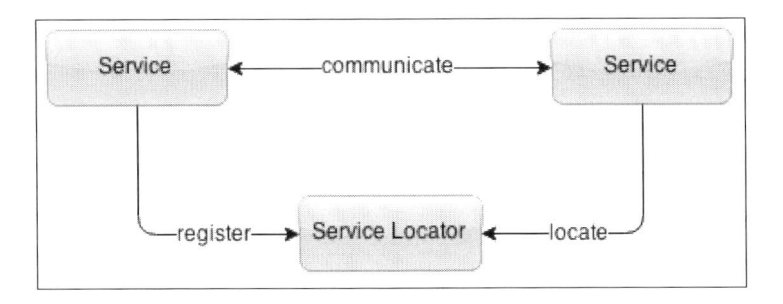

- The **Service Locator** pattern is the concept of abstracting access to a service by the use of a central registry, called the service locator, that allows services to register and get to know each other's access methods. Although this pattern involves adding an extra layer between the components of an application, it can give adaptation and scalability to it.

  There are a couple of advantages to this approach, the most important being the possibility to adapt to the workload. The service locator can control access to the registered services and, if you have several instances of the same service spread across servers, this locator can rotate access to every one of the instances, making it possible to add more instances of the same service and handle more load. Another great advantage is the possibility to unregister services and register new ones with better performance or bug fixes, giving you the possibility to keep zero downtime.

Not everything is good news, however; there are some disadvantages that have to be weighted. The service locator can potentially become a single point of failure, which is something that no one wants. Security is also important, and service registration must be handled with caution to prevent outsiders from hijacking the registry. Also, as services are decoupled from the service locator and the application, they act as black boxes and it might get harder to handle errors and recover from them.

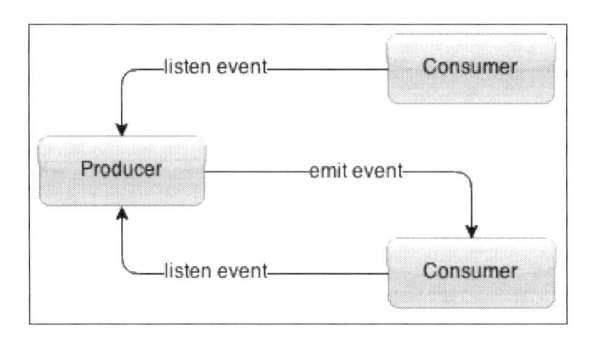

- The **Event-driven** pattern is a pattern that promotes production and consumption of events. This architecture forces the programming logic to react to events. An event is a state change, for example, when a network connection is established, data arrives, or a file handle is closed. An object that needs to be notified of an event (called a consumer) registers (listens) for an event in an appropriate event emitter object (the producer). When this object detects state changes related to it, it notifies (emits) the events to the consumers.

  Events can have data information. For example, if a file reader object is an event emitter, it will probably notify consumers when the respective file is opened, when it has data from the file (whether it is complete or not), when the file is closed (no more data), and if any error occurs eventually (no access permission or filesystem being two examples). The data event could eventually get the file itself and the error event should get the associated error.

  Building applications around this pattern usually makes them more responsive because these systems are, by design, targeted at unpredictable and asynchronous environments, which exist in the case of any system that uses the network or the filesystem. This architecture is extremely loosely coupled, as an event can be almost anything and anywhere, making this pattern scalable and distributable.

  Frameworks with this pattern normally allow developers to create their own products, the event emitters, with custom events and data, extending the core functionality and making it possible to make the entire application event-driven.

# Creational patterns

Creational patterns are the patterns that developers use when creating new data or objects. These patterns give your application the flexibility to choose when to instantiate new objects or reuse current ones. In this type of pattern, you can find some of the patterns that are described as follows:

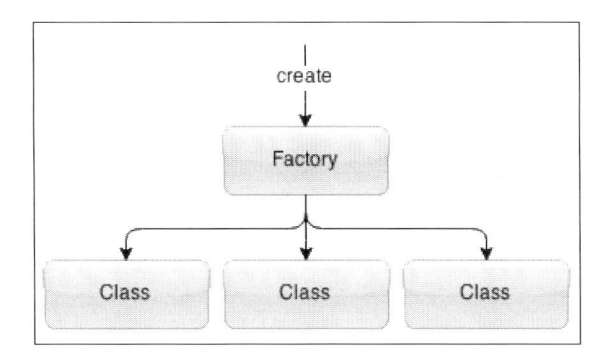

- The **Factory** method pattern is used to abstract the application from specific classes. It is used to create new objects. In this pattern, a method is called, a new (or reused) object is returned, and the logic of the creation (if needed) is handled by another subclass. This pattern is specifically useful when the component that needs to create the new object might not have all of the necessary information (for example, database information) Another use case is when this object is reused across components, the code necessary to create the object might be too complex, and duplication of many pieces of code may be required. Again, a database connection or another data information service access is a good case for this pattern.

- The **Lazy initialization** pattern is when you delay the creation of an object or the calculation of a complex expression. This is also called lazy loading. This pattern is usually seen with the factory method when you save an instance after you call some factory function so that you can later return that very instance when the function is called again. This is another way of getting a singleton.

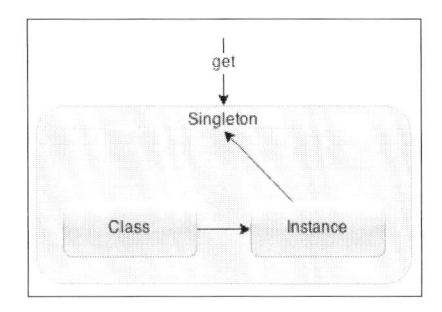

- The **Singleton** pattern is used when a single object instance is required or desired for your application to work efficiently. This pattern is usually made in the class itself, where the developer of the class creates a method to create a new instance, and if an instance was previously created, it is returned instead. It can also appear inside the Factory pattern, where the application might have a library for creating a database connection pool and would prefer that all the modules use the same pool instead of creating new ones. This is especially important for web applications where you want to avoid connecting to the database every time a request comes in. It is also used, for example, in the Active Record pattern, when the same row is needed by several components, and instead of returning different objects, the same object is returned.

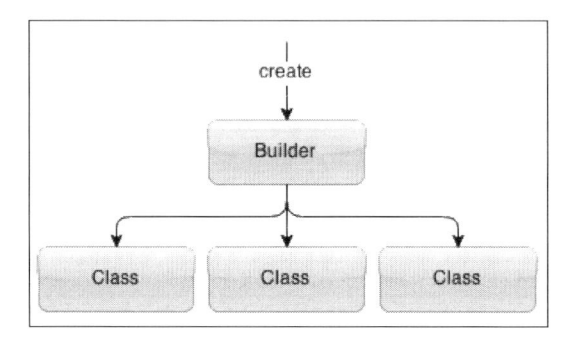

- The **Builder** pattern is a class that is responsible for creating new instances of other classes. This is similar to the Factory method pattern — more flexible but also more complex. A developer normally starts with the factory pattern and it evolves into this pattern. This is especially useful when abstracting a class with several constructing combinations, for example, when constructing a database query.

    The classes behind the builder are usually complex, and the builder sometimes addresses this complexity by exposing simpler methods and evolving as the need arrives. It's a good pattern, where you can cascade or chain the methods to create a more fluent interface.

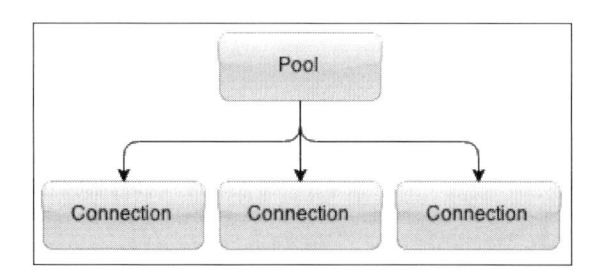

- In the **Object pool** pattern, a set of objects, called the pool, is kept ready for use by other components. This pattern is usually associated with connection pools and other operations that might involve significant initialization time. Usually, such pools are initialized at a lower value (reduced pool size) and grow as per the demand to a higher or limit value.

  This pattern is frequently used in database connections, as they may be expensive to create, considering connecting and authenticating. Always keeping a few connections alive drastically reduces the initialization time and improves performance.

# Structural patterns

Another type of pattern is the structural type. In this type, there are patterns that help in relationships and communication between components. These are commonly used to connect third-party modules together as a common interface. Examples of this type are described as follows:

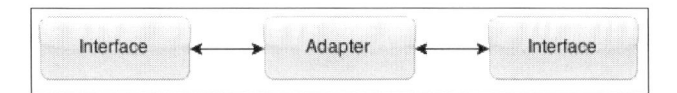

- The **Adapter** pattern is the most common pattern, where two components that are not compatible are connected by a common interface. One rule to distinguish this pattern from similar patterns is that the adapter that connects the two components should not have any logic and should only allow the two interfaces to connect in a new common interface.

  This pattern shows up when you have two interfaces and one needs to be refactored, and the interface will change the methods. While you don't have to refactor the other interface, you'll need an adapter to keep your application running.

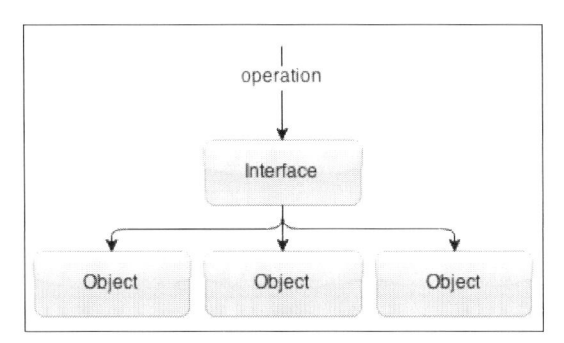

- The **Composite** pattern is used when a group of objects or a single object should be treated and accessed in the same way. This pattern should be used when components don't know when accessing a group of objects or an individual object. It is particularly useful when the complexity of code that is meant to treat the two variations are: an element or a set of elements is not much. Examples of this pattern appear in jQuery and other libraries that treat groups of elements the same as a single element.

  An easy way of creating this pattern is by always assuming a group of objects. If the interface supports a group, it should be fairly easy to check the input and convert a single object into a group of objects before continuing. In this way, the user of the interface won't need to care about it. It's always a good pattern when you make your interfaces more tolerant to user input.

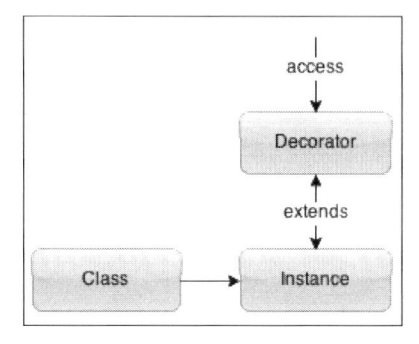

- The **Decorator** pattern is used when a functionality is added to an object without affecting the behavior of other objects of the same class. It is actually the base of prototypal inheritance, which is a fundamental principle of JavaScript. This is achieved by wrapping the object in another class, saving a reference to it, and adding the new functionality to the new class. You use this when a module you want to use does not have all of the functionality you want, and you decide to wrap it and give extra methods. This is an extension, or the next step, of the Adapter pattern. It's common that you find a module that almost fits your needs, but then you realize that there are one or two missing features, so instead of looking for another module (maybe because you're used to it already), you just decorate the first.

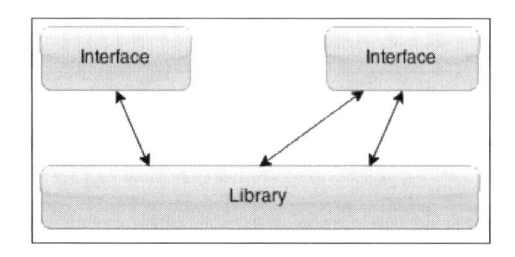

- The **Facade** pattern is in place when you wrap a complex library in an interface easier to use and understand. Sometimes libraries become very versatile with many different options and this pattern is used when you create a less versatile but simpler interface to a complex library.

  This pattern appears when a couple of repeating or complex tasks are common and you decide that it's better to have an interface to do it. It's not an adapter pattern since it's not an interface change; it's a simplified interface. You can see this if, for example, you have a class that understands and talks SMTP. You need to send an e-mail and prefer to have a single method to send a message than a log of complex methods of the original class.

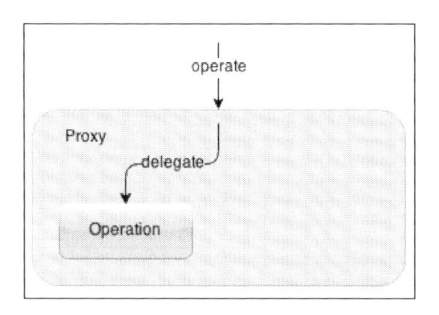

- The **Proxy** pattern, normally used to simplify a more complex task, is a pattern where an object acts as a proxy to access something. It can be another object, a file, a folder, or some database information. This pattern is used, for example, to add a security layer to something else, as it can restrict how and when the application will access a specific resource. An example of this pattern is a REST interface to a service.

# Behavioral patterns

Behavioral patterns are characterized by identifying communication patterns between objects. They classify kinds of behavior and how objects communicate. Some of the most common types are described as follows:

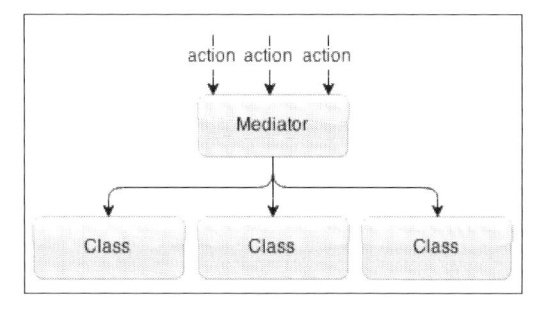

*Development Patterns*

- The **Mediator** pattern creates an abstraction layer, called the mediator, that handles communication with multiple classes. As your application becomes complex, the need for a mediator to lower the complexity of communication between classes arises. This mediator encapsulates communication with all the classes, reducing dependency and lowering coupling by keeping objects from interacting directly with each other. If your application is modular and different modules can be loaded at runtime, this can be called — kind of — your internal API.

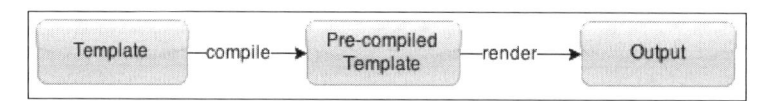

```
Template  —compile→  Pre-compiled Template  —render→  Output
```

- The **Template** method pattern is used by several frameworks. It is usually a method that takes a set of options and compiles part of your information, leaving placeholders to some modifiable parts. This is used, for example, as a way of precompiling a graphic user interface view, leaving some placeholders, such as internationalization text, and eventually some code logic to be run later. This pattern is very effective when some part of the template doesn't change, reducing the time to compile from the template every time it's needed. This is also a typical example of **Inversion of Control**, where it's the template that can call parts of your application instead of your application calling the methods of the template.

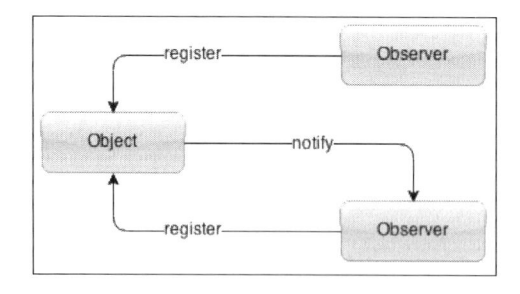

```
              —register—→  Observer
Object  —notify—→
              —register—→  Observer
```

- The **Observer** pattern maintains a list of dependents, called observers, and notifies them of the changes by calling a method provided by each dependent. This is commonly called an event system, and it's used in event-driven architectures, such as Node.js. This pattern is very effective and useful in asynchronous programming. On the other hand, if not properly used, it can cause memory leakage when an event listener is not properly deregistered and the observer keeps a strong reference to it, preventing garbage collection from disposing it (the lapsed listener problem). This pattern is heavily used by the Node.js platform and it is essential that you embrace and understand it if you want to create a performant application.

# Event-driven architecture

Developing in Node.js is no different from other languages. You have some more or less native patterns, widely adopted and fully supported. One very common pattern is **event-driven architecture**. This pattern promotes production and consumption of events. This means that your code should be reactive to events instead of constantly trying to detect changes. Usually, many listeners can consume an event. There are some variations, such as having a way of stopping the event propagation or only allowing the first listener to consume the event, but normally all listeners will be able to consume all the events that they're listening to.

This pattern is very effective when you need to communicate inside your application in a *one to many* module of your code, as it gives you a very lose coupling. This is specifically interesting in **service-oriented architecture** (**SOA**) as it ensures your application components (your services) remain loosely coupled and can be upgraded over time without affecting other services. Imagine you have an application with many services attached and a service called **Sessions**, responsible for managing user sessions, creating them, and destroying them. This service may eventually produce events when sessions change. In this way, other services may listen for the events and act accordingly. This means that a service that only wants to know when sessions are created can, for example, just listen for the create event, and another service that only needs to know when they're destroyed can listen only for that specific event. Other services can then be added without having to change much of your application. This is also good for somehow creating a boundary between services when, for example, you don't want to trust third-party services.

There are some related patterns—sort of variations of this pattern. One widely used pattern is the publish-subscribe pattern. One widely used and very similar pattern is the publish-subscribe pattern. Instead of events, you have messages; instead of listeners, you have subscribers; and instead of event emitters, you have publishers. The main advantage of this pattern is that it's usually implemented to work using the network layer, and so it can be used by services to communicate with each other over the Internet. However, this pattern is actually not that simple and can get quite complex compared to Node.js core events, as it allows message filtering, in which subscribers can decide what kind of messages they want to receive based on message attributes.

Usually, this pattern involves a third element, which is responsible for accepting publisher messages and delivering them to subscribers. This element can possibly scale and allow a more distributed architecture. On the other hand, as it decouples publishers and subscribers, publishers can lose the ability to know who is subscribed to which channels. Also, be aware of the message delivery, because the network layer can introduce many complications and slow down your workflow. This is not something you would want to depend on.

An event-driven architecture allows you to create an application in which the flow of information is determined by events. This is great but there are two things you shouldn't forget:

1. Be careful not to create a kind of deadlock when your flow is expecting an event and it's never triggered or you've registered to listening too late. Usually, this is not fatal to your application, usually, this is not fatal to your application as you're not blocked waiting for the event, but your application will be in an intermediate state from where it can't get out and will probably be leaking memory. From the user perspective, your application is failing.

2. Always handle errors gracefully; don't ignore them. Core modules such as `http` and `net` throw exceptions when you don't properly handle error events. This means that an uncaught exception will be triggered and your application will stop fatally. You're not listening and ignoring uncaught exceptions, right?

Overall, this is a nice generic pattern that fits perfectly into the Node.js platform, and is very handy when you need to communicate between several parts of your application. Also, the language itself, JavaScript, handles this pattern quite well by supporting anonymous functions, called closures.

## Streams

You might have noticed that events and streams are somehow related in Node.js. This is not by accident; it helps make a great workflow that is simple to understand and adapt. Streams use events to inform consumers about the data available for consumption and when the data reaches an end.

One way of looking at streams is to look as if they were Unix pipes (https://en.wikipedia.org/wiki/Pipeline_(Unix)). The goal is to be as useful as piping data across commands to read data, process it, transform it, and then output it. Streams are a fast and easy interface for creating readable, writable, duplex, and transform streams. Let's look at the different types of streams, as follows:

- **readable**: This is, for example, a file parser that reads some kind of format, such as CSV, and emits data events for each line. This stream can be piped to other types of streams. A readable stream can be in flowing mode, which means that data is piped as it becomes available at the source, and the paused mode where data has to be fetched manually when needed (and if available).

- **writable**: Writing to a file or responding to a client are examples of this type of stream. Other examples are data compression streams (`zlib`) and cipher streams (`crypto`). This stream writes data to the destination and informs of its progress. It can also handle what it's called back pressure, when data is being written to the stream and it's not being handled in the opposite side, forcing the stream to keep data in memory.
- **duplex**: This is both a readable and writable stream, as it handles both the source and the destination. Examples of this type are sockets and, again, compression and cipher streams, depending on the objective.
- **transform**: This stream is an extension of a duplex stream where you perform some kind of data transformation between the source and the destination. Compressing data is a good example of this type, but so is converting data between different formats.

# Buffers

Another important piece of the puzzle in the Node.js platform is the buffer. Since JavaScript strings are encoded in Unicode, binary data might get scrambled in the process. Buffers are an alternative to manipulating binary data. As a bonus, you get several methods to read and write numbers in different sizes, whether big or little endian.

Because of binary compatibility, the core modules use buffers in stream data events. Streaming a file to a client or receiving a file from a client and writing it to the disk is as simples as piping streams. And they just work because they pass buffers to each other.

# Optimizations

Using patterns improves your application, as you use well-proven and well-tested concepts that help developers to better understand and eventually improve your code. But improving your code doesn't end here. There is another type of pattern that varies from language to language, and we call it optimization.

An optimization is a pattern that is not specific to any problem but specific to a code structure. The idea is to change the code to be more efficient or to use less memory or other types of resources while doing the same thing. The goal of an optimization is not to get simpler code or to make it more readable. It can be bigger but still readable. Don't optimize for the sake of optimizing and reducing your code readability.

As Node.js uses the V8 engine as the language processor, we have to use V8-specific optimizations in the code. Some optimizations work across versions, others not so much and the effort of optimizing might be worthless. This is because V8 is constantly improving and Node.js platform ships new versions with every release, so an optimization that was good yesterday because of bad performance of V8 on some aspect might not be worthwhile tomorrow when V8 fixes that performance issue. Now let's take a look at some optimizations that are worth noting.

## Hidden types

JavaScript has dynamic type. This means that a variable has a type that is dynamic, and so it can change from, say, a number to a string and vice-versa. This feature is hard to optimize at compile time, and V8 has a feature called **hidden types** where it shares optimizations between objects of the same type. For example, when you create an object using the new keyword, if every instance of the object does not undergo changes in its prototype, they all share the same hidden type and will use the same optimized code:

```
function Person(first_name, last_name) {
  this.first_name = first_name;
  this.last_name  = last_name;
}

var john = new Person("John", "Doe");
var jane = new Person("Jane", "Doe");

// john and jane share the same type

jane.age = 18; // jane no longer has the same type as john!
```

This might not be achievable for complex objects, but for simpler objects, you can enforce it by just setting the properties in the constructor and then sealing the object to avoid any more changes.

## Numbers

Again, since JavaScript has dynamic type, the numbers can change the type. The compiler will try to infer the type, and as soon as it knows it, it will tag the variable to that type in order to be able to perform operations with other variables. Changing the type after that is possible but expensive, so it's better to avoid changing number types. More specifically, avoid getting in and out of the 31-bit signed integers:

```
var number = 32; // 31-bit signed integer
number /= 10; // double precision floating point
```

# Arrays

Arrays can have a variable length; it is changeable over time. For handling this, the compiler has some internal types for each specific type of Array, and switching between these types is not desirable. Arrays should have contiguous keys, starting from zero. Avoid deleting elements in the middle and accessing elements you didn't initialize before. Similar to numbers, you should keep your Array elements in the same type. Also, if you know the size of an Array, you should point it out in the constructor:

```
var a = new Array();
a[0] = 32;
a[1] = 3.2; // internal conversion
a[2] = false; // another conversion
```

In this specific example, it would be better to initialize all the elements up front to allow the compiler to know the hidden type before creating it, instead of inferring it twice.

```
var a = [ 32, 3.2, false ]; // much faster
```

# Functions

Functions inherit from objects, and so the hidden types apply here too. Polymorphic functions will degrade performance substantially. If you want the best performance possible, create a separate function for every constructor you need:

```
function add(a, b) {
    return a + b;
}

add(2, 3); // looks like monomorphic
add("john", "doe"); // it's now polymorphic
```

Similarly, some uses of `arguments` are a performance killer. Avoid reassigning them (for example, when undefined). Instead, use another variable. You should only use arguments to check arguments length and look at a valid index:

```
function add(a, b) {
    if (arguments.length == 1) b = 0; // penalty
}
```

## The for-in loops

There are some performance penalties when using evaluating code in runtime is another feature loop, and for the best performance possible, you should avoid it and use a normal `for` loop. The performance penalty comes from edge cases where the compiler just can't optimize. Always use `Object.keys` to get a list of keys in an object and then iterate that list:

```
var keys = Object.keys(obj);
for (var i = 0; i < keys.length; i++) {
    // obj[keys[i]]
}
```

## The infinite loops

You should never create an infinite loop (`while (true) {}` or `for (;;) {}`). This is a rule of even greater importance for performance code. It's very hard to optimize an infinite loop, and it is preferable to refactor your code and review your logic.

## The try-catch blocks

The try-catch blocks are important in order to be able to capture exceptions, but in an asynchronous architecture, they can be a bit less important. The compiler has difficulty in optimizing the scope inside try-catch, so you should try to move as much of your code out of the statement as you can.

## Eval

Eval is another feature avoidable at all costs, as any function scope with an `eval` call will make the function unoptimizable. Never use this feature unless you really need it, and if you need it, put it in the smallest function possible.

> **Downloading the example code**
>
> You can download the example code files from your account at http://www.packtpub.com for all the Packt Publishing books you have purchased. If you purchased this book elsewhere, you can visit http://www.packtpub.com/support and register to have the files e-mailed directly to you.

# Summary

Developing should be a great experience. Performant applications require some restrictions on how they are designed and developed. Knowing most of the common patterns helps choose wise paths for your application and avoids some performance penalties in the future. However, patterns are not all, and a solid understanding of what's behind the Node.js platform really helps you reach a few levels up on the performance scale.

Even after choosing good patterns and doing the best at developing using some of the optimizations tips described in this chapter, the application can perform poorly on some scenarios. Don't optimize unless you need it. Follow the patterns and the tips, but don't think excessively about it until you test your application performance and realize that you need to optimize it.

# Garbage Collection

When writing applications, managing the available memory is boring and difficult. When the application gets complex, it's easy to start leaking memory. Many programming languages have automatic memory management, helping the developer to forget about this management by means of a **Garbage Collector** (**GC**). The GC is only a part of this memory management, but it's the most important one and is responsible for reclaiming memory that is no longer in use (garbage), by periodically looking at disposed referenced objects and freeing the memory associated with them.

The most common technique used by GC is monitoring reference counting. This means that GC, for each object, holds the number (count) of other objects that reference it. When an object has no references to it, it can be collected, which means that it can be disposed and its memory freed.

In V8, the Node.js engine, this reference counting is not constantly checked. Instead, it's periodically scanned, and this task is called a cycle. Usually, this cycle is not atomic which means that the program will pause execution while this cycle is running. Also, just to keep this reference counting, GC needs memory. This means a memory overhead on your program besides the memory used by the program. Also, because the language is dynamic and objects can change type, memory sometimes is not used in the most efficient way. Recall the previous chapter about development patterns for a more efficient memory usage.

## Automatic memory management

GC tremendously simplifies language usage, giving developers more time to focus on other aspects of the application. Also, it can reduce, although not completely remove, a type of error called memory leaks, which haunt long-lived applications and services. However, there's a performance penalty associated with its periodic task. It can be noticed, or not, depending on how much memory is used and disposed in short periods of time.

By moving memory management out of the developer, Node.js removes or substantially reduces a few types of bugs:

- **Dangling pointer bugs**: These occur when memory is freed but still there are one or more pointers referencing that the memory blocks. If the memory is reassigned, these pointers can cause unpredictable behavior if used to change blocks from other parts of the program. You would have, in this case, more than two places in the application changing the same memory block. This is a particularly difficult bug to find.

- **Double free bugs**: These occur when memory is freed once and then freed again. In between, it might have been reallocated and used by another part of the application, destroying access to a reused block. This is similar to the previous memory, where two places manage the same block, but in this case, one is trying to use it and the other will just wipe the data.

- **Memory leaks**: These occur when objects are dereferenced before being freed. This happens when a program allocates memory, uses it, and then disposes the reference to that memory before explicitly freeing it. This type of bug can leave to memory exhaustion if this behavior occurs repeatedly, especially on long-lived services.

- **Buffer overflows**: These occur when trying to write more information than the space allocated to the task. This is quite common when, for example, a program allocates a memory block somewhere after it needs more space than the memory it allocated, and fails to detect and reallocate the required space. This bug can halt the application or service.

On the other hand, moving memory management away from the developer removes a great deal of control over memory usage and how it's managed. GC will consume resources when looking at the memory being used and deciding what and when to free unreferenced objects, creating unpredictable pauses during your application execution. Also, the time at which the GC starts doing its job may be unpredictable and out of your control, which can introduce unpredictable performance penalties over times when your program is in need of resources.

This is the case of Node.js, but since it uses V8, which exposes a `gc()` method under the `--expose_gc` flag, you can manually force its use. You cannot decide when it will run, but you can force it to run more often if you think it's best. You can also tweak some of GC's behavior. To find out more run the `--v8-options` node.

There's no way of blocking its use, so you can just make it run more often, perhaps reducing its footprint. The GC's cost is proportional to the number of referencing objects, so if you use this method after substantially reducing referenced objects, you can keep your application lean and reduce the GC penalty later.

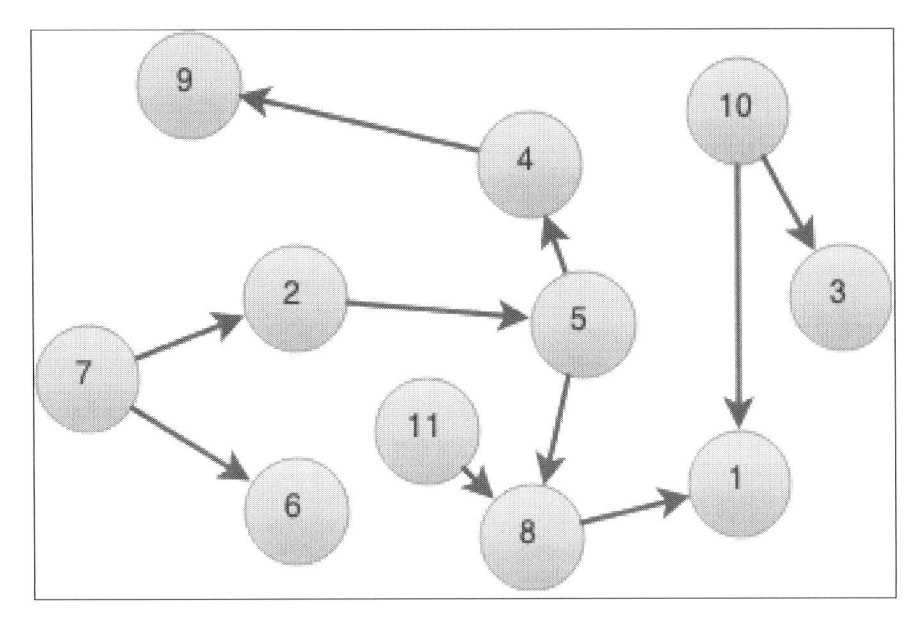

Figure 1: GC memory graph

## Memory organization

Think of memory as a mesh of elements, usually primitives (numbers and strings) and objects (hash tables). It can be represented as a graph of interconnected points. Memory can be used to hold object information or to reference other objects. You can look at this interconnection as a graph where leafs are elements that hold information and the other nodes are references to other nodes (in Figure 1, nodes **1**, **3**, **6**, and **9** are leafs).

When working with V8, there's some terminology you may find useful to better understand V8 Inspector or Chrome Developer Tools. The memory used by the object itself is called **shallow size**. It's used to store its immediate value, and usually, only strings and arrays can have a significant size.

There is also the distance column, which is the smallest graph distance from a root node to the node itself. A root note is a node from where references start pointing other nodes. In Figure 2 it would be node **2** as there's no arrow pointing to **2** and everything on the graph starts on node **2**. In Inspectors, you'll see another term in **Profiles** called **Retained size**. This is the size that will be freed once the object is deleted. It is at least the size of the object plus the size of the referenced objects, which will also be freed immediately since they will also get unreferenced. Confusing? Let's see an example:

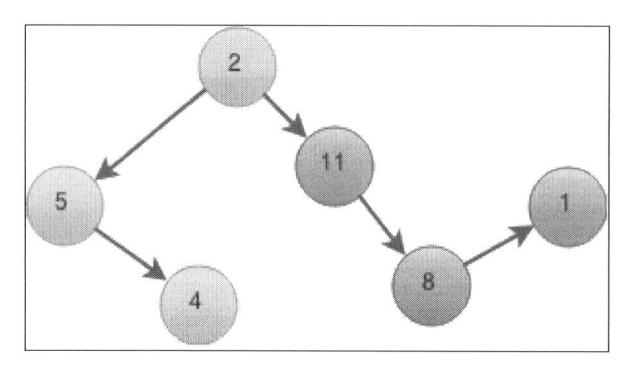

Figure 2: GC-marked nodes before sweep

In the preceding diagram you see that node **2** is the root node in the graph, as there's no node referencing (pointing to) it. This node references node **5** and node **11**. If the reference to node **11** is removed, then there's no path from node **2** (and the rest of the left part of the graph) to get to nodes **8** and **1**. These nodes are part of the retained size of node **11** as they're useless without it. When node **11** is removed, they'll be removed too.

# Memory leaks

A memory leak is a continuous loss of available memory, and it occurs when a program repeatedly fails to release the memory that it's no longer using. Node.js applications can suffer from this issue indirectly because of the GC. It's usually not the GC's fault, but is caused by some object destruction that is not taking place when it should, and this is not that difficult when you're using an event-driven architecture.

Leaks haunt every developer as soon as their application hits medium size. As soon as your program starts having more interactions with external elements like other programs or clients, or when your program complexity grows, you start leaking memory. This happens when, for some reason, you're not dereferencing a no-longer-useful object of your application. If the GC finds that the object is still referenced by other objects, even if it's no longer useful to your application, it will remain in the heap and will be moved to a place called **old space**.

Usually, objects live for a very long period of time (since the beginning of the application) or for a very short period of time (serving a specific client). The V8 GC is designed to take advantage of these two most common types of objects. GC cycles usually clean these short-lived objects, and if it thinks that these objects are still useful (that is, when it survives more than one or two GC cycles), it will move them to a bigger zone, where it will start to accumulate garbage. When this zone gets bigger, the GC cycle duration gets bigger too and you'll start noticing some stalls (complete breaks in the application) for a second, or even a few seconds. If this happens, it means you're already late at analyzing your application.

For a large memory limit, such as the default 1 GB limit of V8, if you're not monitoring your application, you'll probably notice leaks when your application starts stalling for a second, and after that, it's a few more seconds before it just stops because of that memory limit. GC cycles become very CPU intensive for large object collections, so you should really monitor GC memory management and, if possible, avoid greater memory usage.

## Event emitters

Since Node.js uses event emitters, there's a question that should be in your head right now. Since GC can only sweep objects that are unreferenced, this means that event emitters will not be collected after you attach event listeners to them:

```
var net    = require("net");
var server = net.createServer();

server.on("connection", function (socket) {
  socket.pipe(socket);
});
server.listen(7, "0.0.0.0");
```

The preceding code is just an example of an echo server. In this example, GC will never collect `server`, which is good in this case since that's the main object of the program. In other cases, you might have such situations where your emitters won't get swept because of references to listeners. Most importantly, event callbacks are functions—extended objects in JavaScript—and won't get swept either.

Take a closer look at the previous example. Imagine that for each client (socket), you had more complex code with some private protocol. To simplify it, you use the Adapter pattern and create an abstraction to access each client. This abstraction could be an event emitter as a means to decouple it from other parts of the application. While your client keeps connected, any event listeners that don't explicitly unlisten events will not get garbage collected even if they are not supposed to exist anymore (this is true even if you null them). And if your connection gets stuck and doesn't time out (for example, a mobile connection), you'll collect a good pack of zombie connections for a while.

# Referencing objects

The main goal of GC is to identify trashed memory. This refers to the memory blocks that you're your application no longer uses, usually because your code no longer references them. Once identified, this memory can be reused or freed to the operating system:

```
function foo() {
  var bar = { x: 1 }, baz = bar.x;

  return bar; // baz is unreferenced but bar isn't
}
```

In the preceding example, although both `bar` and `baz` are local variables for the function (because of JavaScript function scoping), `baz` will be deference after `return` but `bar` won't, and it will not be freed until you completely deference it. This might look obvious, but if your application grows and you start using external modules that you don't know how they work internally, you might get more dangling references than you expect:

```
function foo() {
  var bar = { x: 1 };

  doSomething(bar);

  return bar;
}
```

Now imagine you call the `foo` function and ignore the returned object. You might think that it'll get unreferenced, but there's no guarantee of that because of what `doSomething` might have done. It might have held a reference to `bar`:

```
function foo() {
  var bar = { x: 1 };

  doSomething(bar);

  bar = null;
}
```

Now imagine you don't need to return the bar variable, and so you null it after you no longer need it, destroying the reference. That's better, right? No! If the `doSomething` function holds a reference to `bar`, there's nothing you can do outside `doSomething` to dereference it completely.

Even worse than this is the fact that the function can create a circular reference by creating a property that references itself in `bar`. But GC is clever enough to figure out when the rest of your application no longer uses an object. It depends on how complex your code is. Remember that if there is a doubt (that is, it's still referenced somewhere and can still be used), GC will not sweep the object.

In each cycle of its job, GC pauses V8 execution in what is called stop-the-world, knowing exactly where all objects are in the memory and what references exist. If there are too many references, GC will process only part of the object heap, minimizing the impact of the pause. The following image shows how V8 scans the memory objects, marks unreferenced ones (first row, in red), sweeps them from list (second row) and then compacts the list by removing empty spaces between objects (third row)

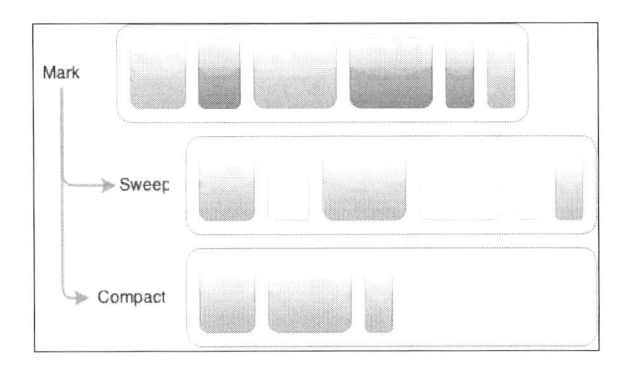

The previous V8 GC generation had two algorithms for cleaning the old space: mark-sweep and mark-compact. In both the algorithms, GC went through the stack and marked reachable (referenced) objects. After that, it could use mark-sweep to just sweep the objects that weren't reachable by freeing their memory, or use mark-compact to reallocate and compress the memory used. Both the algorithms worked at the page level. The problem with these two algorithms was that they introduced significant pauses in medium sized applications.

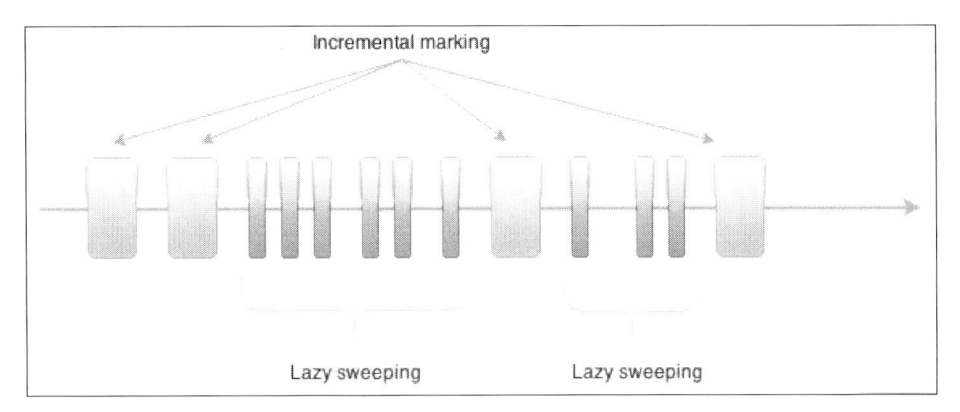

In 2012, Google introduced an improvement that significantly reduced pauses in garbage collection cycles. It introduced incremental marking to avoid traversing a possibly huge zone. Instead, GC just goes through part of the zone to do the marking, making the pause smaller. Instead of a big pause, GC makes more pauses but small ones. But the improvement does not end here. After marking, GC does what is called a **lazy sweep**. Since GC knows exactly which objects are referenced and which are not (because of the previous mark step), it can now free the memory of the unreferenced ones (sweep). But it doesn't need to do that right away. Instead, it just sweeps on an as-needed basis. After sweeping them all, GC starts a new mark cycle again.

GC is fast as long as your program is kept lean and simple. Don't create a monolithic monster and then look for a way of raising the memory limit of V8. On a 64-bit machine, you can almost double the 1 GB limit, but that's not the solution. You should really split your application. Even so, if you're thinking about changing the limit, the option in the node executable you're looking for is `--max-stack-size` (in bytes).

## Object representation

In V8, there are three primitive types: numbers, booleans and strings. Numbers have two forms: SMall Integers (SMI), which are 31-bit signed integers, or normal objects in situations such as doubles (big numbers) or numbers with extended properties. Strings also have two forms: one is inside the heap, and the other is outside the heap, with a wrapper object on the heap as a pointer to it.

There are also other objects such as arrays, which are objects with a magic length property, and native objects, which are not in the heap itself (they're wrapped like some strings) and are therefore not managed or swept by GC.

## Object heaps

GC stores objects in an object heap. The heap is divided into two main zones: new space and old space for—you guessed it—new objects and old objects respectively. New space is where objects are created and old space is where objects are moved to if they survive one or more GC cycles. Since GC is not constantly working, between cycles, objects can be created and they can be destroyed (and dereferenced) a few moments later. This is the most common object behavior, so GC usually sweeps them efficiently. Other objects live longer, and so they will survive cycles since they keep being referenced and used. This is where memory leaks can show up.

These two spaces are designed with different goals in mind. The new space is smaller than the old one and is designed to be fast, meaningful, and analyzed by the GC very quickly. The old space is larger and contains objects moved there after a cycle. This old space can grow to a very large size, from a couple of megabytes to a gigabyte. This design takes advantage of the common behavior that most objects have a short lifetime and so live only on the new space, which is smaller and faster to manage.

Each space is composed of pages, contiguous blocks of memory that hold objects. Each page has a couple of headers on top and a bitmap telling GC what parts of the page the objects use.

This separation of objects and movement from one space to the other introduces some problems. One is, obviously, reallocation. Another is the need to know whether the references to an object in the new space are only in the old space. This is a possible situation and should prevent the object from being cleaned, but this would force GC to scan the old space to figure it out, breaking the speed of this architecture. To avoid this, GC maintains a list of references from the old space to the new space. This is another memory overhead but it's faster to scan this list. It's usually small since it's relatively rare to have this kind of reference.

The new space is small, and it's cheap to create new objects since it's just a matter of incrementing a pointer in the already reserved memory. When this new space gets full, a minor cycle is triggered to collect any dead objects and reclaim the space, avoiding the use of more space. If an object survives two minor cycles, it is moved to the old space.

In the old space, objects are swept in a major cycle that is less frequent than the minor one in the new space. This major cycle can get triggered when a certain amount of memory is reached in this space or after a more prolonged period of time. This cycle is less frequent and can stall the application for a little longer.

# Heap snapshots

V8 allows you to get a heap snapshot to analyze memory distribution across objects. It allows you to see what objects your code uses, how many of each are used, and how the application uses them if you request heap snapshot dumps over time. There are several ways of collecting a heap snapshot, and we'll look at some of them.

*Garbage Collection*

Let's create a small leaking program and analyze it with the `node-inspector` module. Open a terminal and install node inspector globally (`-g`) so that you can use it anywhere in your machine. In the following example, we're using `sudo` since global modules usually reside in a restricted area:

`$ sudo npm install -g node-inspector`

The inspector needs to compile some modules, so you'll need a compiler. If it installs correctly, you'll see a list of installed dependencies and you can now start it. Once it's running, there's no need to restart it while you change and restart your program. Just start it now with no parameters and leave it in a terminal tab:

`$ node-inspector`

You should see something similar to the following console output. You can see that I'm using version `0.10.0`, but you might get a different version. For the purpose of the example, it's not actually critical that you use the same version. Depending on the version you use, the output may vary. In this case, it is something similar to this:

```
$ node-inspector
Node Inspector v0.10.0
Visit http://127.0.0.1:8080/debug?ws=127.0.0.1:8080&port=5858 to start debugging.
```

Open your web browser and head to the page indicated in the output. Now let's create a program called `leaky`. The purpose of this program will be to leak memory intentionally. Create a folder and inside install the V8 profiler:

```
$ mkdir leaky
$ cd leaky
$ npm install v8-profiler
```

Be aware that this module can also need a compiler. Now, in the same folder, create a file called `leaky.js` with the following content:

```
require("v8-profiler");
var leakObject   = null;
function MemoryLeak() {
  var originalObject = leakObject;

  leakObject = {
    longString : new Array(1000000).join("*"),
    someMethod : function () {
      console.log(originalObject);
    }
  };
};

setInterval(MemoryLeak, 1000);
```

The program can be confusing, but the idea is to blind GC from seeing that we're forcing it not to garbage-collect objects, and so, leak memory. If you look more closely, you will see that `leakObject` gets redefined with a function that outputs it if called, but the way it references it makes GC unaware of our awful goal. Be aware that when running this program, you'll starve the memory quite quickly, perhaps in the order of 100 megabytes per second. Run this with debug turned on:

```
$ node --debug leaky.js
```

Now head over to the web page you just opened, click on **Refresh**, go to the **Profiles** tab on the page, choose **Take Heap Snapshot**, and click on the **Take Snapshot** button, as shown here:

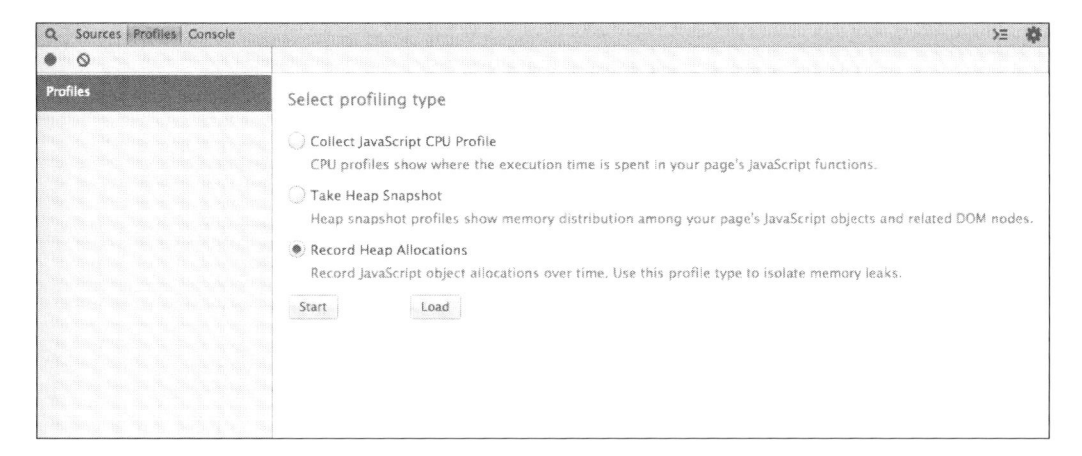

Wait a minute and hit that button again. You'll see snapshots appearing on the left sidebar and you'll notice that they don't have the same size. They're growing and it's GC leaking our nonsense program. You can easily notice this if you select the last snapshot and choose to compare it with the first one.

*Garbage Collection*

You'll see that there's a delta change in both size and the new objects. A positive delta means that more objects were created than destroyed.

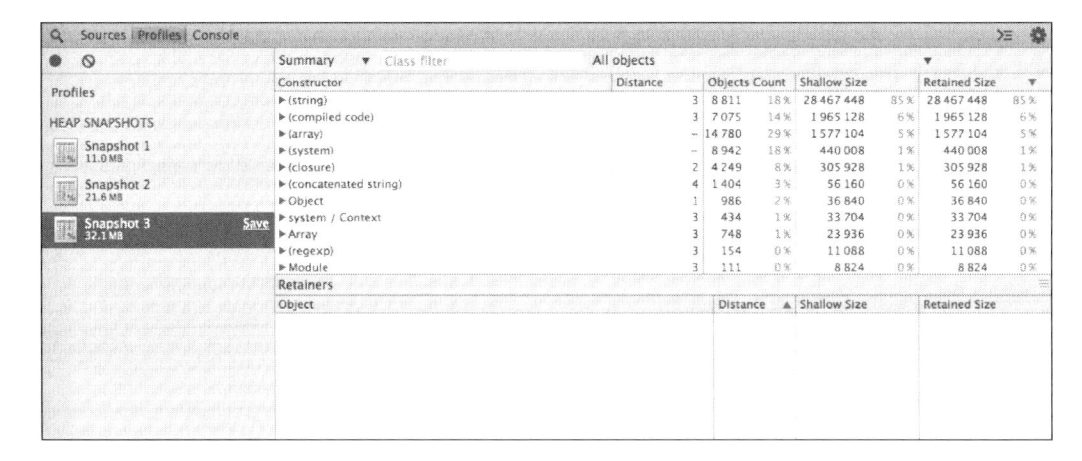

You can see in the preceding screenshot what the inspector looks like when showing a snapshot. There's a list of constructors or base objects. In this case, since we're comparing **Snapshot 3** with **Snapshot 1**, there are columns that show how many objects were created and deleted as well as how much memory was allocated and freed.

Another useful method for detecting memory leaks is recording object allocations over time. Using this very inspector, restart the program, head to **Profiles**, choose **Record Heap Allocations** and hit **Start**, as shown in this screenshot:

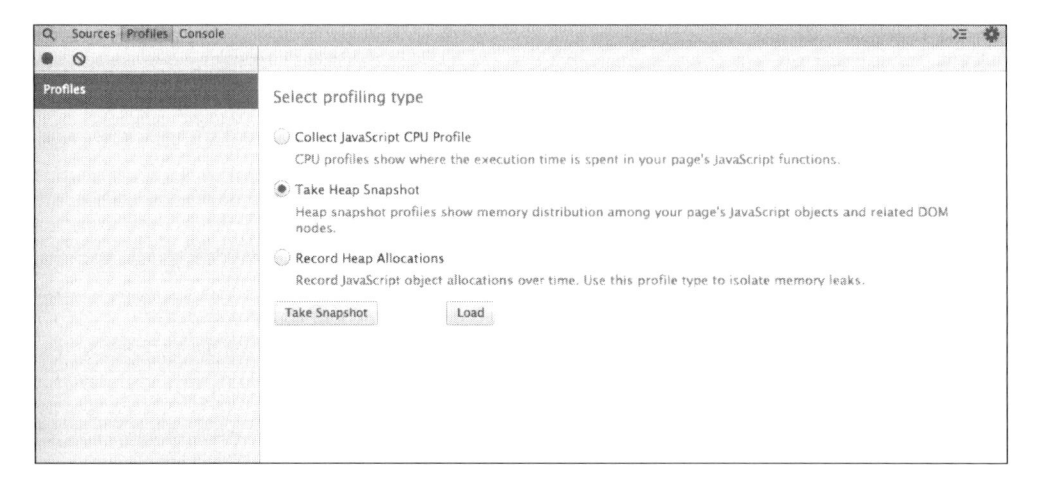

The inspector will start recording. It will stop when you click on the red circle in the top-left corner. You'll see a growing timeline and a bar chart for allocations for every minor cycle. If you wait a bit, you'll see major cycles and object reallocations (from new zones to old zones).

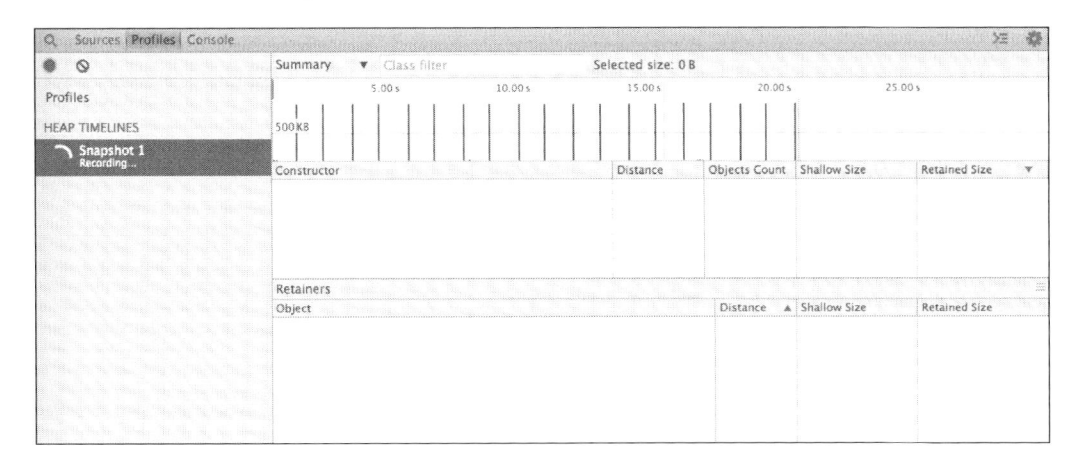

After stopping, you can select a period of time by clicking on a start point and dragging it to the end point. You'll see only the allocations in that period, not all the objects. You can save the snapshot for later analysis or comparison. In this specific example, you can see how memory is quickly being consumed every second.

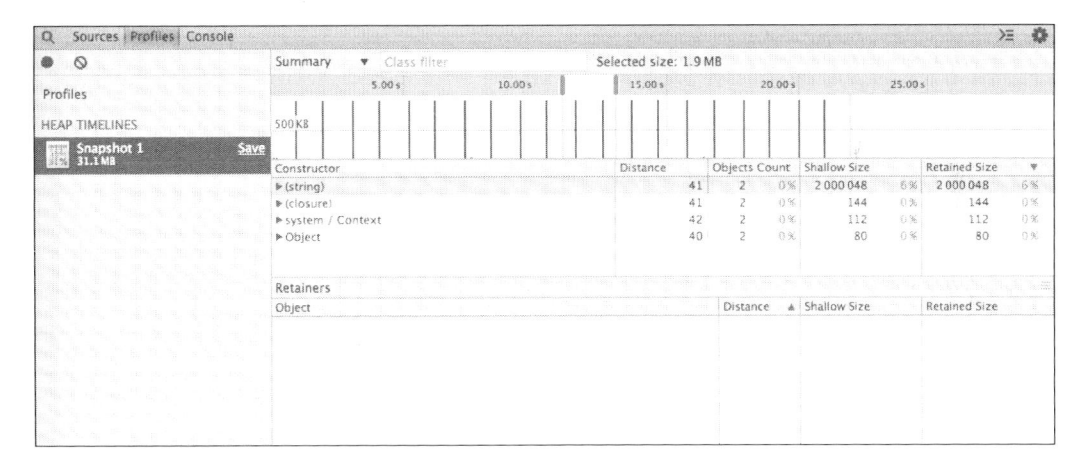

# Garbage Collection

You can click and expand the objects list to look at every object. If you're looking for a particular object, you can use the filter at the top. In this example, you can open the (string) group and you'll see there are several instances like \*\*\*\*\*\*\*\*... that we created in our program.

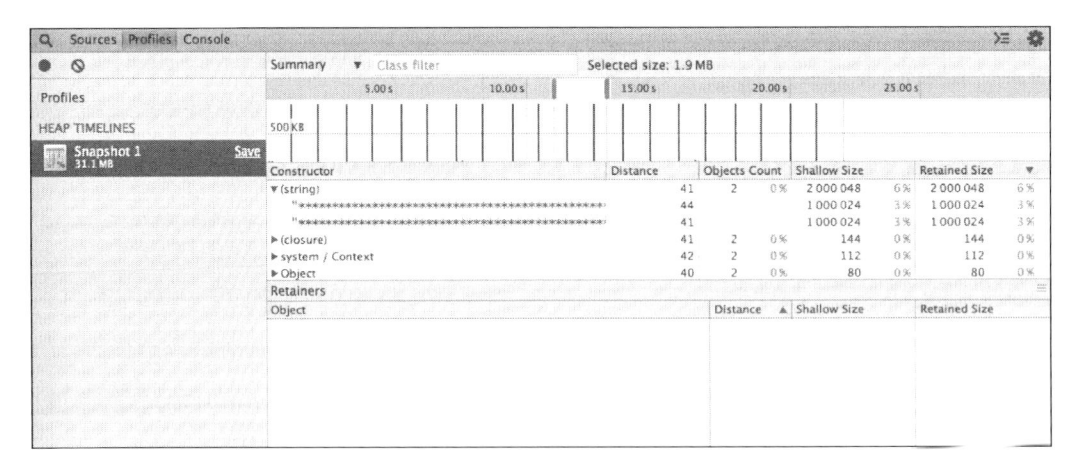

Using `v8-profiler` allows you to do more than just debug with `node-inspector`. You can, for example, take snapshots of your code and analyze it—maybe compare it with previous snapshots—or serialize and save it for later analysis.

For example, taking the previous program example into consideration, we can periodically check how many nodes are there in our stack:

```
var profiler   = require("v8-profiler");
var leakObject = null;

function MemoryLeak() {
  var originalObject = leakObject;
  leakObject = {
    longString : new Array(1000000).join("*"),
    someMethod : function () {
      console.log(originalObject);
    }
  };
};

setInterval(MemoryLeak, 1000);
setInterval(function () {
  console.log("mem. nodes: %d", profiler.takeSnapshot().nodesCount);
}, 1000);
```

If you run this new version, you might get an output similar to the following. This is a proof that objects are surviving GC cycles and leaking memory:

```
$ node --debug leaky.js
Debugger listening on port 5858
mem. nodes: 37293
mem. nodes: 37645
mem. nodes: 37951
mem. nodes: 37991
mem. nodes: 38004
mem. nodes: 38012
```

This is just an example. If you monitor your application and the memory keeps growing over time while it is idle (not doing anything), it is a reason to analyze further. The first-class citizens (so-called classes, for people coming from other object-oriented languages) will appear in the constructor list of the snapshots of your application.

There are other modules you can use to analyze and monitor your Node.js program memory and garbage collector. The `heapdump` module is another simple module that can help you just dump a heap snapshot every now and then to disk. Keep in mind that these snapshots are synchronous, so your program will pause for a moment if the heap is large.

To use it, just install it like the other modules previously installed:

```
$ npm install heapdump
```

Then change your program to use it. Here's an example of a program that takes a snapshot to disk every minute. This is not a real or good use case, but perhaps a hourly snapshot with some kind of disposable script to avoid filling your disk might not be a bad idea:

```
var heapdump = require("heapdump");

setInterval(function () {
  heapdump.writeSnapshot("" + Date.now() + ".heapsnapshot");
}, 60000);
```

The name of the file is the Unix date in milliseconds, so you will always know when it was taken. Run it and wait for at least one snapshot to be written to disk. In this case, you don't need to enable `debug` in the node (`--debug`).

# Garbage Collection

You kept `node-inspector` running on the terminal, right? If not, please do it. Then go to its web page, as you did before, and refresh the page.

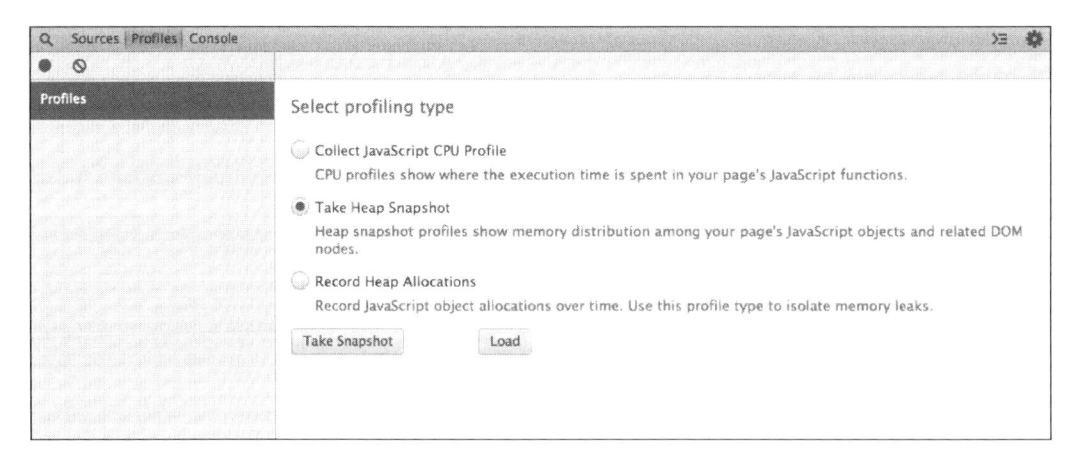

Now, instead of choosing **Take Snapshot**, just click on the **Load** button and choose the snapshots from your disk. This is another approach—an offline one—and it is usually more useful since you're usually not running your code in debug mode and looking at it live in v8-inspector. Also, `node-inspector` will restart the interface when your program stops, so you need to save your snapshots before restarting node-inspector.

If you have a memory leak you know of and you are able to reproduce it by just stressing it, you can use this approach and perhaps add a little twist to the execution of the program by activating GC trace lines for every action. You can then see when GC is sweeping or marking. The following is an example of what you'll see if you monitor the GC actions:

```
$ node --trace_gc leaky.js
[26503]        8 ms: Scavenge 1.9 (37.5) -> 1.8 (37.5) MB, 0.8 ms
[26503]        9 ms: Scavenge 1.9 (37.5) -> 1.9 (38.5) MB, 0.9 ms
[26503]       53 ms: Scavenge 3.6 (39.5) -> 3.2 (39.5) MB, 0.7 ms
[26503]      116 ms: Scavenge 5.1 (40.5) -> 4.1 (41.5) MB, 1.9 ms
[26503]      155 ms: Scavenge 5.9 (41.5) -> 4.4 (41.5) MB, 1.1 ms
[26503]     1227 ms: Scavenge 14.3 (50.1) -> 14.5 (50.1) MB, 0.8 ms (+
1.6 ms in 1 steps since last GC) [allocation failure].
[26503]     1235 ms: Mark-sweep 14.6 (50.1) -> 5.4 (43.5) MB, 6.7 ms (+
1.6 ms in 1 steps since start of marking, biggest step 1.6 ms) [HeapSnaps
hotGenerator::GenerateSnapshot] [GC in old space requested].
```

Part of the previous output was truncated for clarity. The number *26503* is the process ID of the program in this example. You can see when the action took place and how long it took at the end of each trace line. You can also see the actions (Scavenge and Mark-sweep) and the memory evolution for each cycle.

For a running application, It's not feasible to have —trace-gc enabled (as in the previous command), and you should think of an approach that works for your architecture. One of the options is using heapdump, scheduling a snapshot every hour or so, and saving the last 10 or 20 snapshot. When using this approach, you should at least look at the last snapshot and compare it with the previous one to see how your application evolves over time. You might find slow memory leaks or very fast memory leaks. For the fast ones, you should be able to record heap allocations and rapidly stop leaks. For slow ones, it's harder to spot it, and only over very long periods are you able to compare changes and find the ghosts.

There's also another useful module that can help you spot leaks, which is called memwatch. This module will look for heap size changes, and when it finds that the heap size is constantly growing, it will emit a leak event (the irony). It also has a nice stats event with information on GC cycles.

Let's change our initial program to use this module instead of any profilers or inspectors. Yes, it doesn't need them, and it doesn't even need you to enable node debug. First, let's install it:

**$ npm install memwatch-next**

Now let's change our program to something similar to this:

```
var memwatch   = require("memwatch-next");
var leakObject = null;

function MemoryLeak() {
  var originalObject = leakObject;

  leakObject = {
    longString : new Array(1000000).join("*"),
    someMethod : function () {
      console.log(originalObject);
    }
  };
};

setInterval(MemoryLeak, 1000);

memwatch.on("leak", function (info) {
  console.log("GC leak detected: %d bytes growth", info.growth);
```

```
});

memwatch.on("stats", function (stats) {
  console.log("GC stats: %d cycles, %s bytes", stats.num_full_gc,
stats.current_base);
});
```

Now simply run the program. Let it run for a few seconds and you'll see something similar to this example output:

```
$ node leaky.js
GC stats: 1 cycles, 13228416 bytes
GC stats: 2 cycles, 7509080 bytes
GC stats: 3 cycles, 7508408 bytes
GC stats: 4 cycles, 17317456 bytes
GC stats: 5 cycles, 23199080 bytes
GC stats: 6 cycles, 32201264 bytes
GC stats: 7 cycles, 45582232 bytes
GC leak detected: 40142200 bytes growth
```

You will notice GC cycles occurring very often. This is because of our program behavior. GC adapts to rapid heap changes and triggers cycles more often. If you change the memory leak call period to 5 seconds or more, you will have to wait much longer to see cycles and leaks.

The memwatch module works by checking heap changes after GC sweeps and compacts it, so it won't trigger a leak just because your application is using memory, but because you're using it and not disposing it.

Another very useful feature of this module is the ability to help you compare heap snapshots. You do this by explicitly telling the module that you want a heapdiff. At this moment, the module snapshots heap, waits for your call to snapshot again, and compares it. After that, it will give you an object showing the totals before and after and the changes to each snapshot:

```
var memwatch   = require("memwatch-next");
var heapdiff   = new memwatch.HeapDiff();
var leakObject = null;

function MemoryLeak() {
  var originalObject = leakObject;

  leakObject = {
    longString : new Array(1000000).join("*"),
```

```
      someMethod : function () {
        console.log(originalObject);
      }
    };
  };

  setInterval(MemoryLeak, 1000);

  setTimeout(function () {
    console.log(heapdiff.end());
  }, 10000);
```

Run the program. After that, you'll get an output similar to the following:

```
$ node leaky.js
{ before: { nodes: 19524, size_bytes: 3131984, size: '2.99 mb' },
  after: { nodes: 21311, size_bytes: 12246992, size: '11.68 mb' },
  change:
   { size_bytes: 9115008,
     size: '8.69 mb',
     freed_nodes: 2201,
     allocated_nodes: 3988,
     details:
      [ [Object],
        [Object],
        [Object],
        [Object],
        ...
        [Object],
        [Object],
        [Object] ] } }
```

If you look at the `change.details` array, you'll notice that you have a list of constructors that have changed between heaps. If you have a leak occurring between the snapshots, it will be in one of those items. In our case, it's the string constructor since we're leaking string variables.

With or without any of these modules, you should definitely monitor memory usage and growth. Rapid memory leaks will starve your resources and leave your clients unhappy. For high-load applications, you should create stress tests to be able to detect leaks before the application goes into production.

## Third-party management

In the spirit of dividing your application into smaller components, sometimes it might be a better idea to move some objects and manipulations to external services, which are sometimes optimized for specific workloads and object formats. Explore some of these servers before starting to manipulate large object structures:

- Memcached for key/values and Redis for lists, sets, and hash tables
- MongoDB if you want to run JavaScript on the data, and ElasticSearch for interesting features, such as data timeout or hierarchical elements (documents inside documents)
- HBase if you need some complex map/reduce code, and Hypertable if you need a lightweight version of that code
- OrientDB if you need a graph database, and Riak to store large binary data

Your application is usually running on memory, so if it fails and stops, the memory used is lost and your precious data can be lost too. Using an external service to handle the data (and sometimes manipulate it) can greatly reduce your memory footprint. Moreover, these services usually allow you to access concurrently, enabling you to split the data manipulation effort for several instances of your application or tool.

## Summary

You now see that the garbage collector task is not all that easy, but it certainly does a very good job managing memory automatically. You can help it a lot, especially if you are writing applications with performance in mind. Preventing the GC old space from growing is necessary to avoid long GC cycles. Otherwise, it can pause your application and sometimes force your services to restart. Every time you create a new variable, you allocate memory and inch closer to a new GC cycle. Even after understanding how memory is managed, you sometimes need to inspect your memory usage behavior. The cleanest way is by collecting snapshot heaps of the memory stack and analyzing using the V8 inspector or other similar pieces of software. The interface is self-explanatory, and leaks will show up simply if you sort the object list by shallow size, retained size, or reference counting. But before creating an application with a huge memory footprint, take a look at databases, whether relational or not, as this will help you store and manipulate the data, avoiding the need to do it yourself using the language. Remember that JavaScript was not designed to create computationally intensive tasks. If you still need to perform more intensive tasks, you might want to instrument the code to analyze and improve it so that you can achieve optimal performance.

In the next chapter, we will see what profiling is, what the benefits of doing it are, some available analysis tools, and how to understand results and upgrade your code.

# 4
# CPU Profiling

Profiling is boring, but it's a good form of software analysis where you measure resource usage. This usage is measured over time and sometimes under specific workloads. Resources can mean anything the application is using, be it memory, disk, network, or processor. More specifically, CPU profiling allows you to analyze how and how much your functions use the processor. You can also analyze the opposite—the non-usage of the processor, or the idle time.

Node.js is not primarily meant for continuous CPU-intensive tasks, and sometimes, for profiling, it is important to identify the methods of the intensive task that are holding to the processor and keeping other tasks from performing better. You may find huge call stacks continuously occupying the processor or repetitive and recursive tasks not ending as you expected. There are several techniques, such as splitting and scheduling tasks instead of continuously running them as they block the event loop.

You may ask why these tasks are so horrible. The answer is simple; Node.js runs around an event loop, which means that when your code ends a specific task, the loop restarts and pending events get dispatched. If your code does not end, the rest of the application will be kept in standby until the task finishes. You need to be able to split a big task into smaller ones for your application to perform well.

The main goal of an application should be to use the least resources possible, so using the least processor time possible would be ideal. This is equivalent to be running most of the time idle in the main thread. This is when the call stack is the smallest possible. From a basic Node.js perspective, that should be level zero.

When profiling the processor, we usually take samples of the call stack at a certain frequency and analyze how the stack changes (increases or decreases) over the sampling period. If you use profilers from the operating system, you'll have more items in the stack than you probably expect, as you'll get internal calls of Node.js and V8.

In the chapter, the following topics will be covered:

- The I/O library
- Fibonacci
- Flame graphs
- Profiling alternatives

# The I/O library

The library used by Node.js to be able to perform asynchronous I/O operations across multiple platform environments is **libuv**. This is an open source library. Actually, It is used by platforms to provide similar functionality to other languages such as Luvit and Lua. **Libuv** is a cross-platform library that uses the best possible methods for each platform to achieve the best I/O performance and still exposes a common API.

This library is responsible for network tasks (TCP and UDP sockets), DNS requests, filesystem operations, and much more. It's the library that accesses files, lists directory contents, listens for socket connections, and executes child processes. The following image shows how Node.js uses V8 and libuv at the same level:

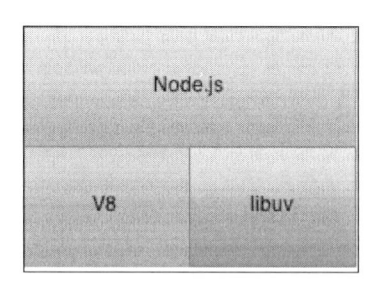

You can see that libuv does not depend on V8 to interact with I/O. It's a C library with its own thread pool. This thread pool is designed to be fast and avoid creating and destroying task threads too often, as they're very expensive. The library handles many I/O tasks from the network to the filesystem. It's responsible for Node.js exposing `fs`, `net`, `dns`, and many more APIs. During an event loop, your code can request I/O data. This is processed, and when ready (that is, all or part of your request is ready for you), it triggers an event that will hopefully be handled in the next event loop. The following image describes how the thread pool works. Your code runs in the event loop (green), libuv runs in separate threads (blue) and triggers events to your code (orange) that get triggered before each cycle:

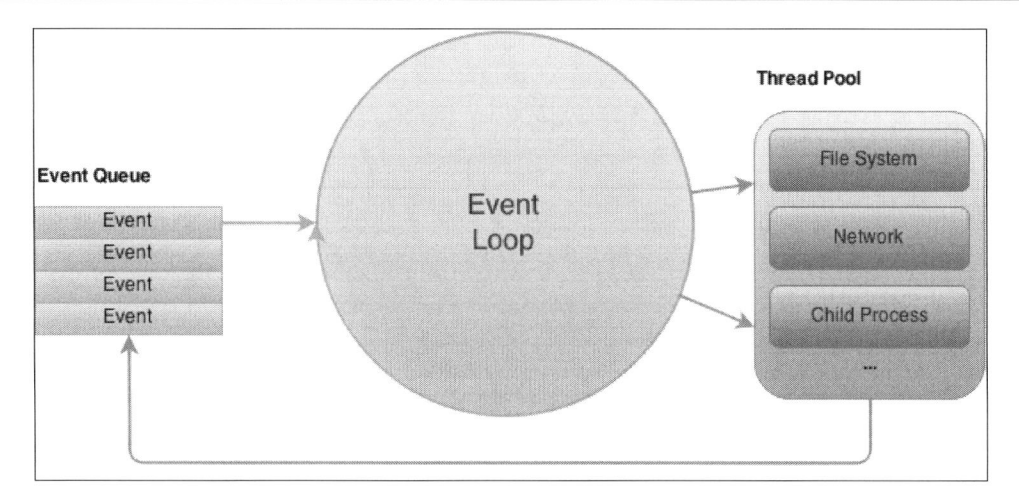

This means that if you request a file's content and start performing a lot of intensive operations, it doesn't affect the file operation since it's done outside your scope. So, although Node.js is single threaded, there are several operations that are done in separate threads (from a pool). This is important to remember as we profile our code so as to differentiate what a Node.js bottleneck, a libuv (I/O) bottleneck, and just a system bottleneck are.

## Fibonacci

Let's dive into an example. Take it with a grain of salt. It's actually a very common and criticized example, involving the Fibonacci sequence. Let's create a simple HTTP server file called `fib.js` that will answer every request with a response based on the sum of the numbers of a Fibonacci sequence of a specific length. There are no dependencies here, just plain Node.js. Additionally, we'll use the `ab` command (Apache Benchmark) to make a few requests to our server. If you have a Debian-based machine, you just need to install `apache2-utils` to be able to use this command:

```
var http   = require("http");
var server = http.createServer();

server.on("request", function (req, res) {
  var f = fibonacci(40);

  return res.end("" + f);
});

server.listen(3000);
```

# CPU Profiling

```
function fibonacci(n) {
  return (n < 2 ? n : fibonacci(n - 1) + fibonacci(n - 2));
}
```

As you can see, the `fibonacci` function is recursive (as it should be), and is called every time a new request comes in. It should not be a surprise to see that this won't perform that well. Let's start it and tell V8 that we want a profile log:

**$ node --prof fib.js**

Now let's benchmark it with just 10 requests with two concurrency connections. The following output has been truncated for clearer understanding:

```
$ ab -n 10 -c 2 http://localhost:3000/
This is ApacheBench, Version 2.3 <$Revision: 1604373 $>
(...)
Concurrency Level:      2
Time taken for tests:   18.851 seconds
Complete requests:      10
Failed requests:        0
(...)
Requests per second:    0.52 [#/sec] (mean)
Time per request:       3822.383 [ms] (mean)
(...)
```

You can see that it took 2 seconds for each request (half a request per second). That doesn't look good, does it? Let's stop the server. You should see an `isolate*.log` file in the same folder. You can open it with V8 Tick Processor. There's an online version (http://v8.googlecode.com/svn/trunk/tools/tick-processor.html), if you want; or if you have the node source as I do, you will find it in `deps/v8/tools/tick-processor.html`.

## Chrome V8 profiling log processor

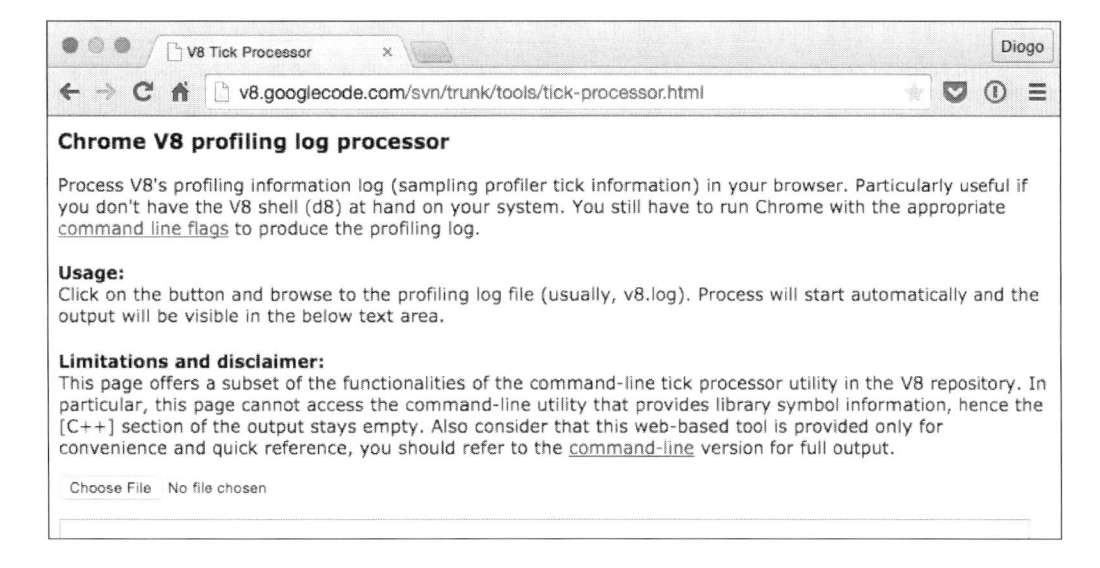

Process V8's profiling information log (sampling profiler tick information) in your browser. Particularly useful if you don't have the V8 shell (d8) at hand on your system. You still have to run Chrome with the appropriate command line flags to produce the profiling log.

**Usage:**
Click on the button and browse to the profiling log file (usually, v8.log). Process will start automatically and the output will be visible in the below text area.

**Limitations and disclaimer:**
This page offers a subset of the functionalities of the command-line tick processor utility in the V8 repository. In particular, this page cannot access the command-line utility that provides library symbol information, hence the [C++] section of the output stays empty. Also consider that this web-based tool is provided only for convenience and quick reference, you should refer to the command-line version for full output.

Click on **Choose File** and pick your log. The tool will chew like process, throw like return output similar to the following. Once more, some of the output has been removed:

```
Statistical profiling result from null, (...).

(...)

 [JavaScript]:
   ticks  total  nonlib   name
   14267  89.1%  100.0%  LazyCompile: *fibonacci fib.js:15:19
       1   0.0%    0.0%  Stub: reinitialize

(...)

 [Bottom up (heavy) profile]:
(...)
   ticks parent  name
   14267  89.1%  LazyCompile: *fibonacci fib.js:15:19
   14267 100.0%    LazyCompile: *fibonacci fib.js:15:19
   14267 100.0%      LazyCompile: *fibonacci fib.js:15:19
   14267 100.0%        LazyCompile: *fibonacci fib.js:15:19
   14267 100.0%          LazyCompile: *fibonacci fib.js:15:19
```

# CPU Profiling

Our `fibonacci` function is really using our processor all the time. You can notice the recursive pattern in the `Bottom up (heavy) profile` section. You can see different levels (indentations) because of the recursiveness of the function.

> Please note that when running your own test, you should restrict running the server to only the time of the benchmark (as in this example). If you leave the server running more than that, the use of your function will get mixed with the idle time.

In our example, it's not easy or even better to split the code because the operation is really simple (adding two numbers). In other use cases, you may be able to optimize some operations by modifying your code using, for example, some of the techniques shown in *Chapter 2, Development Patterns*.

Another way of improving performance in this case is by using a technique called **memoizing**. What this does is wrap a function and cache its return value based on the arguments. This means that a function, for a specific set of parameters, will only be called once, and then the return value will be cached and used repeatedly. Of course, this does not apply to every situation. Let's try it on our server:

```
var http   = require("http");
var server = http.createServer();

fibonacci = memoize(fibonacci);

server.on("request", function (req, res) {
  var f = fibonacci(40);

  return res.end("" + f);
});

server.listen(3000);

function fibonacci(n) {
   return (n < 2 ? n : fibonacci(n - 1) + fibonacci(n - 2));
}

function memoize(f) {
  var cache = {};

   return function memoized(n) {
     return cache[n] || (cache[n] = f[n]);
   };
}
```

[ 60 ]

There are modules that help you achieve this result. In our case, we're adding a `memoizing` function and actually overwriting the function with itself—memoized. This is important because the function calls itself recursively, and so it really needs to be overwritten.

This will cache every call to it, so only the first `fibonacci(40)` call will not use the cache. Moreover, since the function calls itself with *n-1* and *n-2*, half of the calls will be cached, so the first call will be even faster. Running an `ab` test will get you very different results:

```
$ ab -n 10 -c 2 http://localhost:3000/
This is ApacheBench, Version 2.3 <$Revision: 1604373 $>
(...)
Concurrency Level:      2
Time taken for tests:   0.038 seconds
Complete requests:      10
Failed requests:        0
(...)
Requests per second:    263.86 [#/sec] (mean)
Time per request:       7.580 [ms] (mean)
(...)
```

This is much better at more than 250 requests per second. This is obviously a bad benchmark because if you increase the number of requests to a couple of thousands, the number will be even better (a couple of thousands). If you use V8 Tick Processor, you will notice that the function call is no longer there:

```
(...)
[JavaScript]:
ticks  total  nonlib  name
    1   0.1%   12.5%  Stub: ToBooleanStub(Null,SpecObject)
    1   0.1%   12.5%  LoadMegamorphic: args_count: 0
    1   0.1%   12.5%  LazyCompile: ~httpSocketSetup _http_common...
    1   0.1%   12.5%  LazyCompile: ~exec native regexp.js:98:20
    1   0.1%   12.5%  LazyCompile: ~UseSparseVariant native array...
    1   0.1%   12.5%  LazyCompile: ADD native runtime.js:99:13
(...)
```

This is obviously a bad and very simple example. Every application is different and analyzing it will involve knowing more about it. Using development platforms helps centralize your knowledge of the subject and helps you improve more easily overtime.

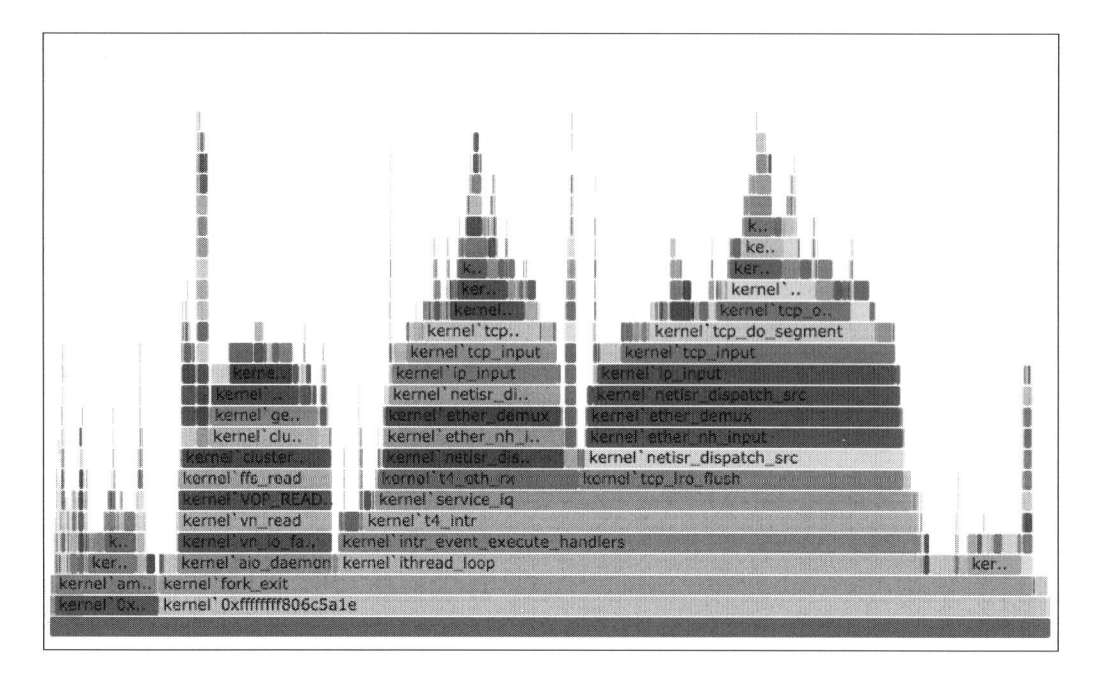

## Flame graphs

Flame graphs are a visualization technique used to profile an application and rapidly and more precisely spot the most frequently used functions. These graphs replace or complement the previous log text output, as they give a more pleasant and simple way of profiling.

A flame graph is composed of several stacked blocks, each representing a function call. It usually shows usage times horizontally (not necessarily in an order). When a function is called by another function, the first function is displayed on top of the former one. Using this rule, you can figure out that the blocks at the top will definitely be smaller (horizontally) than the ones at the bottom. This creates a graph that visually resembles a flame. Moreover, the blocks normally use warm colors (such as red and orange), so the graph really looks like flames.

These can be used with different objectives, such as seeing memory usage and leaks. For example, you can create a flame graph to see how the CPU is being used (A busy CPU is one that is working hard, nonstop. An idle CPU is one that is doing nothing). Another good use is to see when your application is idle and I/O is very slow compared to CPU and memory, it's normal when applications block (stop) waiting for a file from disk or from the network. This is called off-CPU. This is better seen in cold colors (blue and green). A mix of the two CPU flame graphs can also give you a good understanding of how your application behaves.

Creating flame graphs is not easy on Node.js yet, and it depends on your system. Since V8 has perf_events support (https://codereview.chromium.org/70013002), I currently find it much easier to do it on a Linux box using the perf command and perf_events, but you have alternatives, such as DTrace (http://www.brendangregg.com/flamegraphs.html). Let's try it right now. Get yourself an Ubuntu machine (or a virtual machine) and install some dependencies. Note that some of them depend on your current kernel version:

```
$ sudo apt-get update
$ sudo apt-get install linux-tools-common linux-tools-`uname -r`
```

Now let's run our node server telling V8 that we want the perf_events output. This time, let's run it in the background so that we can see its PID more easily, and run perf afterwards:

```
$ node --perf-basic-prof fib.js &

[1] 30462
```

There's the PID we need—30462. Then let's run perf to collect events for about a minute. The command will not return until it finishes (listening for events for a minute), so you need to open another console to run the benchmark command:

```
$ perf record -F 99 -p 30462 -g -- sleep 60
# on another console..
$ ab -n 1000 http://localhost:3000/
```

# CPU Profiling

We're telling perf to record events with a frequency of 99 Hz for the 30462 process, enabling call graphs (-g), and do this for 60 seconds. After that time, this command should end. The first version of code is so slow that will take longer than 60 seconds to finish so the user can stop it after a minute. The second version is much faster and there's no need to do it.

You can look at the directory and notice that there's a perf.data file. Now we need to tell perf to read this file and display the trace output. We'll use it and convert it into a flame graph. For this, we'll use a stack trace visualizer created by Brendan Gregg. This output will be converted into an SVG file. You can then open it in your favorite browser. First let's get this stack output:

```
$ perf script > stack01.trace
```

Now let's download the stack trace visualizer and use it to convert this file. You'll need git to get this command:

```
$ git clone --depth 1 http://github.com/brendangregg/FlameGraph
$ ./FlameGraph/stackcollapse-perf.pl < stack01.trace | ./FlameGraph/flamegraph.pl > stack01.svg
```

You should now have a `stack01.svg` file that you can interact with. You can click on a horizontal block to zoom into that level or click on the lowest block to reset zoom. For the first version of your server, you should get something similar to this graph:

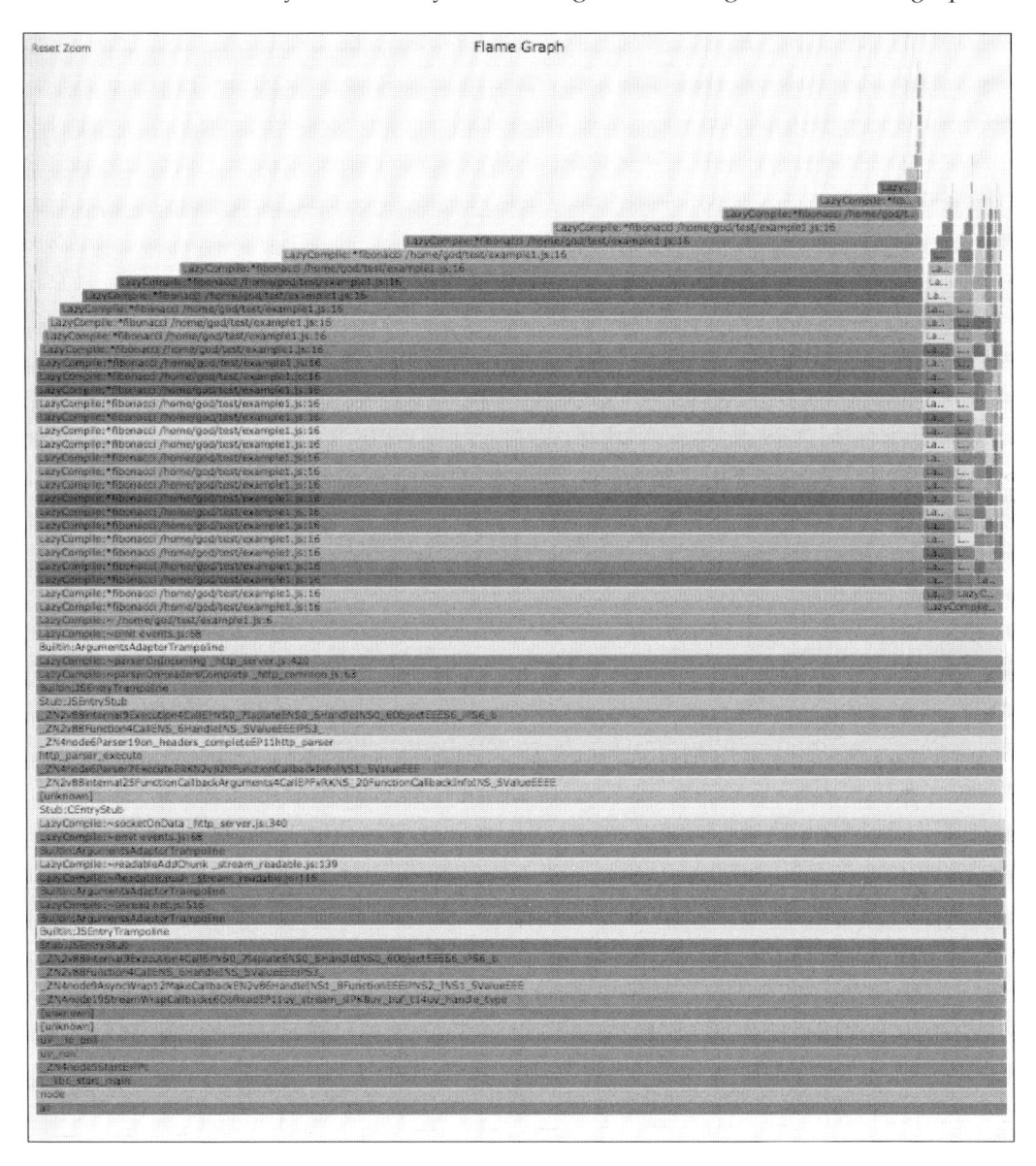

# CPU Profiling

You can clearly see the recursive pattern that is pushing the flames higher. There's an initial big flame and there are others next to it. If you click on the base of the second flame, you'll see something similar to the following:

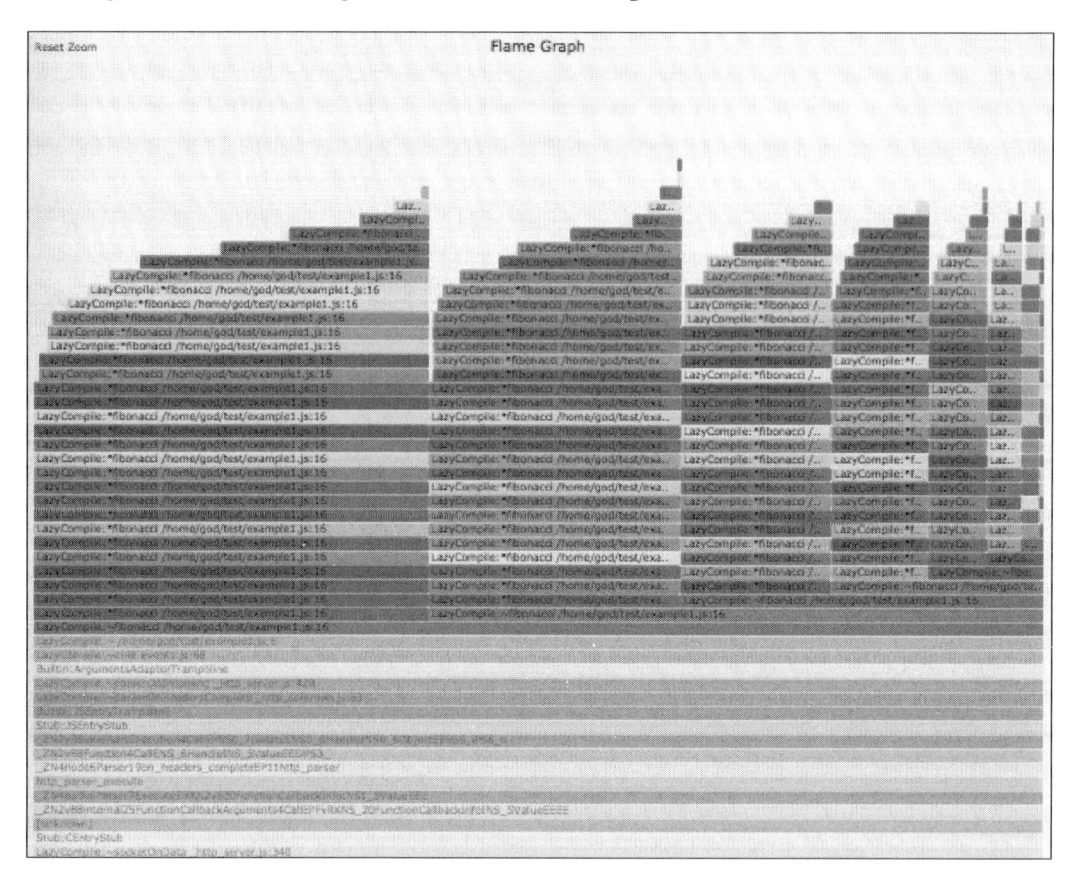

Now you can clearly see your processor being exhausted by this inefficient and recursive function. When inspecting the flame graph, take a look at the bottom line. It will display the information we saw in the initial outputs of the log processor, such as usage percentage.

If we are using the second server version, we'll need to increase the benchmark load if we want to see anything useful. Try creating the flame graph for the second server version using the following steps:

```
$ node --perf-basic-prof fib.js &
[1] 30611
$ perf record -F 99 -p 30611 -g -- sleep 60
# on another console..
```

```
$ ab -n 10000 http://localhost:3000/
$ perf script > stack02.trace
$ ./FlameGraph/stackcollapse-perf.pl < stack02.trace | ./FlameGraph/
flamegraph.pl > stack02.svg
```

Now open this new SVG in your browser and see how the flames are thinner. This means that although the stack size may be large, the duration of that stack size is short. Something similar to this is more normal:

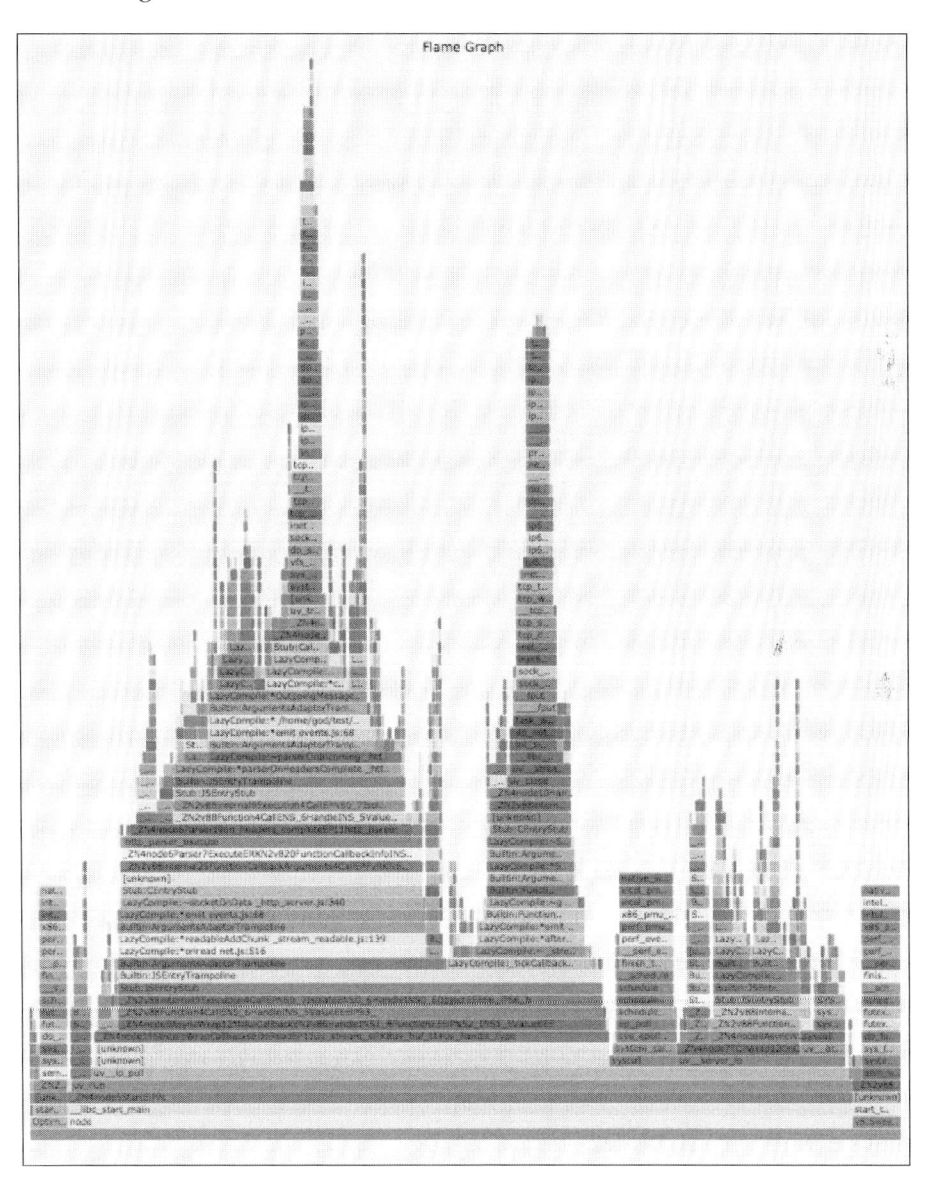

At the bottom of the graph, you'll always see `node` or `main` as Node.js spends most of the time on the main thread. On top of the node or main, you'll see other lines. Every stacked line means a call by the line below. As you reach the top of the flame, you'll start seeing actual JavaScript code. You'll find many calls to the internal functions of Node.js related to events and the `libuv` tasks.

> As a rule of thumb, a flame graph with a huge and wide flame means excessive CPU usage. A flame graph with high but thinner flames means low CPU usage.

## Profiling alternatives

There are other alternatives for profiling your application's processor usage depending on the operating system. You can try DTrace if you use a supported system. I won't recommend using it just yet on a Linux box. Moreover, if you're not using an Illumos-based system, you might just forget it, at least for Node.js. Linux has more call stack debugging tools that you can use to log stacks and then produce a flame graph.

Node.js has profiling modules and even call stack trace modules, but I recommend that you avoid debugging them at the language level and go for the operating system level. It's much faster, is less intrusive to your code, and usually gives you a bigger picture of the behavior, or bad behavior, that you're trying to profile. Remember that the system is not just your application and there can be other factors outside your stack scope that influence your performance.

You can use flame graphs for other types of data. For example, you can trace device I/O `calls` or `syscalls`. You can filter a trace to specific function calls to see when and for how long a function is used. You can trace memory allocations, and instead of gathering allocation calls, you can gather the allocation size in bytes. There are many uses for this type of graph, as it can be really handy for visually analyzing your application behavior.

## Summary

In environments seen nowadays, it's very important to be able to profile an application to identify bottlenecks, especially at the processor and memory levels. Systems are complex and divided into several layers, so analyzing processor usage using call stacks can be really hard without some tools and visualization techniques, such as flame graphs. Overall, you should focus on your code quality before going for profiling.

As you saw in our example, a simple and effective solution for our server was to cache the results. Caching is a very important technique and is usually crucial in balancing resource usage. Normally, you have available memory and it's better to cache a result for a small period of time than to process it every time, specially when the result is imutable.

Next, we'll look at how you should use and store your data and how, when, and for how long you should cache it. We'll take a look at the pros and cons of some cache methodologies so that you can be more prepared to choose your own path to making your application the most performant application possible.

# 5
# Data and Cache

Data is one of your most important assets in your application. Actually, it should be the fundamental asset. You might run your application anywhere, but without your data, it is pointless. By data, I mean the information that your application manipulates, generated or not by your end users. If your application can't work without a database, that database has an important piece of data that you must preserve.

Application data is very important. In web applications, users access it using the Internet and their data is stored on the server side, this importance increases. As your user base grows and the total size of your data increases, it becomes even more important to plan how your data is stored and how it's used.

And don't forget to have a backup plan. You wouldn't want to lose your data and have no way to roll back, even if the rollback means going one week back in time. Your users might accept losing some data (1 week), but will definitely not accept losing everything.

Let's take a look at data storage by looking at some important topics:

- Excessive I/O
- Database management systems
- Caching data and asynchronous caching
- Clustering data
- Accessing data

# Data storage

There are many ways of storing data. It depends on what type of data you have and how big it can become. If you just need to store a simple key/value pair, you can use a file with the format of your choice (for example, an INI or a JSON file). If that key/value pair grows to thousands or millions, you probably won't want to keep it there. You need to think about your data and choose the best possible storage for it, at least from your viewpoint.

If you have other applications, you might try to choose the same data storage to all or some of those applications. This is actually not a bad decision. Choosing the second best tool and trying to use just one or two tools for a couple of applications greatly improves your chances of gaining knowledge about that subset, instead of using the best tool for every application and ending up with many tools and little knowledge about each one.

# Excessive I/O

When using a custom solution, we need to carefully plan how we store and access our data, especially when and how many times we do it. Your host has a disk throughput limit and you wouldn't want to reach it. Also, you'll certainly not want to read your data from the disk every time you need it. It can work during your local tests, but if your application is targeted to thousands of users, it will break and you might start receiving `EBUSY` or `EMFILE` errors.

One of the strategies is to avoid excessive I/O to just read it at start, manipulate it in the memory, and flush the data to disk from time to time. Data can be stored in a variety of formats, **JSON** being the most famous and used as of now. This has the disadvantage of forcing your application to implement a single channel to read and write to the file or else you'll get corrupted data sooner or later.

Instead of creating your custom data storage, use databases or other data model servers. Leave data storage to professionals and focus on your applications. Some advantages of this are as follows:

- Data storage does not need to be maintained
- Database servers are optimized for high-performance scenarios
- Database servers normally support having more than one machine holding the data, allowing your application to scale in size as you need it

It all depends on the system you choose. It's better to take your time and pick a good one before you start. I would focus on scalability and consistency. Speed is something you can't measure, and it varies from application to application and from use case to use case.

# Database management systems

If you choose a **database management system** (**DBMS**), it's very important that you be comfortable with it. Don't put a server that you're uncomfortable with in production, as you'll definitely regret it. When using a DBMS in production, you need to be comfortable with:

- **Management**: It's very important that you be able to replicate your application scenario to a new host without thinking too much about it. You should know how to initialize your storage and manage access. Look for visual interfaces (such as desktop and web) and avoid managing only through a console; you'll make more mistakes in a console as it's harder for complex tasks. Visual interfaces usually have automation tools and can help you avoid syntax errors.
- **Security**: Be careful about default permissions, especially localhost permissions, as they're usually set as permissive and give full control over the data. You don't want to lose data, right?
- **Backups**: It's critical that you have a scheduled and automated plan and that you know how to roll back to a backup. You should run trials on another host. You wouldn't want to roll back just to find that your backups are corrupted. Install a cron job (either locally or remotely), export it from time to time, and try it out. I personally prefer to have one or two backups that work rather than have 10 that don't.
- **Structure**: Knowing how you can organize and correlate your data for better storage and faster access is mandatory. You definitely don't want to make changes later.

The data structure you choose is directly related to your DBMS and your application's performance. Make a sketch of your data and see how your data entities relate with each other. It's quite common to have several tables in your database. After all, that's one of the reasons you use a database in the first place.

What you usually don't think about is that you probably have a single table, maybe a history table or similar, that over time will represent more than 90 percent of your database space usage. It is critical that you optimize that table and decide whether there are columns you don't need or you can move to another table. You can thank me later!

Even after optimizing that table, you won't be able to stop its growth. Do you really need to have a lifetime history or can you export data monthly or yearly to another format and wipe it from the database? Having a database that can grow and even expand to multiple servers is good, but that isn't a synonym for performance.

With respect to this matter, analyze what you might value the most. Is it integrity? Do you need extra security? Do you plan on splitting the database across different servers, as MongoDB is able to? Do you prefer a mature server that has been proven to be stable or will you opt for a new technology? As I said before, try the second best choice. You'll probably be able to use it more often and avoid getting a lot of different technologies that will be harder to maintain.

Your data should be structured by now. For example, if you're creating a calendar application, you probably have entities such as users, calendars, and events. After creating the basic structure, you'll probably realize that you need more structures to relate calendars with users (maybe access permissions) and users with events (maybe participants). After a couple of development iterations, you'll probably have more.

Your structures will grow and your tables will start getting more columns. You'll realize that in this case, your bottleneck table is the one that holds events. Hopefully, it will not be too late to optimize it and remove some columns that are rarely used and can be moved to another table. When there's no space left to reduce, you have to think about other options.

# Caching data

Caching becomes relevant when a piece of information is requested too often and its value will not change, for example, historic values. It's a good method of improving performance if these values require some complexity and manipulation in the database. Even if they're not historic values and can change, sometimes caching is not that bad, at least for a couple of minutes.

In complex systems, you may find cache as the second level of abstraction between the application and the database. In such cases, bidirectional updates happen; that is, data is fetched to the cache and when changed by some user action, the cache data is updated and then the database is also updated. This is faster than clearing the cache and forcing a new request to the database to fetch the data that we already know. You may find this in basic applications, for example, in session data.

Some databases can perform this caching, but others don't, and you cannot rely on them to do it. Also, in other cases, they can't cache because you need to manipulate the data. In some cases you need to address caching to another application or another key/value service that you can use to save values and use them for a while. Redis can be used as a caching service. It supports some nice features, such as complex structures, transactions, and time-to-live keys.

Your cache logic should be something similar to this:

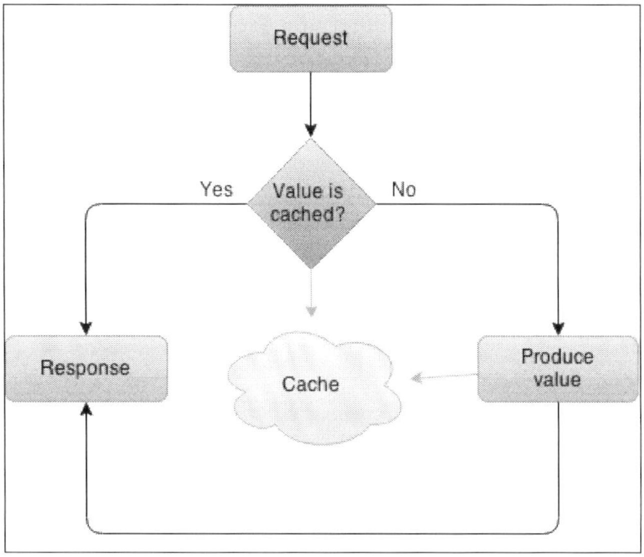

[Flowchart: Request → Value is cached? → Yes: Response; No: Produce value → Cache → Response]

This logic can be used in a variety of ways. You can use a cache in memory, getting the fastest cache possible for small sets. If you know that your cached data may exceed your available memory, you can use files. This happens if, for example, you generate image or document thumbnails. You can cache them, and probably, the best location to store them is the disk.

You can use services that handle data storage and allow you to focus on your application logic. Some of the most popular and simple services to work with are memcached and Redis. There are pros and cons for each of them. In both cases, they need zero setup to start using them.

# Asynchronous caching

Writing Node.js applications forces you to think asynchronously. This means that you'll face some challenges, a few of which you probably don't even know yet. One particularly painful challenge is asynchronous caching. It doesn't matter whether you're using an external service or a simple internal function; the asynchronous part is on your side and is the one responsible for giving you unpleasantness.

# Data and Cache

The problem won't show up easily; you might figure it out just when the load gets high and you see a lot of cache function hits. This is not simple to describe, so let's look at a fake example of a cache that we probably do somewhere in every application:

```
var users = {};

function getUser(id, next) {
  if (users.hasOwnProperty(id)) {
    return next(null, users[id]);
  }

  userdb.findOne({ id: id }, function (err, user) {
    if (err) return next(err);

    users[id] = user;
    return next(null, user);
  });
}
```

It's very incomplete but you get the idea. Every time you want a user, you call `getUser`. This function will get it from somewhere (`users.findOne` might be from an ORM) and return it. Then it will store it in a hash table, and if you request it again, it will return that user directly. There's no time to live or proper error handling, but that won't solve the next problem.

We're assuming that fetching the user is very quick, right? Imagine it takes some time, a few seconds maybe. Next, imagine that this function is used very often. What happens if fetching the user takes, for instance, 10 seconds because of some hiccup in the network and, in that time, you call this function 100 times?

There's no cached value and each one of the 100 calls will try to access the database because they ignore that the first call will actually cache the value and the rest of the 99 calls could use it. If the problem is in the user fetching, it will accumulate calls and drop your application to the ground. This happens because fetching the user is not instant, and so the following calls to the same user should be queued until the user is fetched.

It could be something like the following code. Again, this is a simplified version:

```
var users = {};

function getUser(id, next) {
  if (users.hasOwnProperty(id)) {
    if (users[id].hasOwnProperty("data")) {
```

```
      // already have a value
      return next(null, users[id].data);
    }
    // not yet, queue the callback
    return users[id].queue.push(next);
  }

  // first time
  users[id] = {
    queue: [ next ]
  };

  userdb.findOne({ id: id }, function (err, user) {
    if (err) return next(err);

    users[id].data = user;

    users[id].queue.map(function (cb) {
      cb(null, user);
    });

    delete users[id].queue;
  });
}
```

Take your time to understand it. As you can see, it's not the paradigm that has pitfalls; it's the way. Usually, developers are trained but not prepared for the asynchronous platform that Node.js (and others for the matter) enforces on you.

For many years, it was good practice (and it still is) to get an abstraction to the database called **Object-relational mapping** (**ORM**). Abstractions create a new layer that allows you to change the database type (more or less) and still keep your application working. This is actually not that simple for a more mature application, as it can be quite difficult to avoid certain specificities of a server in order to improve performance. Besides this small advantage, it can reduce access speed and so make your application a little slower. It has other advantages, however, especially in the professional market, as you can apply your business model and entities directly to your code.

For historic data or a big dataset in general, ORMs are not exactly the best option. Many ORMs give you extra power over every item but that comes with a cost (speed and memory). For a big dataset, you get extra power (and big speed and memory cost). You'll figure out that it's not just the layer that's turning your application slow; it's also the database, which is usually not ready for huge datasets in a table (huge means gigabytes).

*Data and Cache*

You may look for other services that can give you intermediate levels of caching and, if used correctly, a sense of performance by helping you reach specific data that you use the most. Services such as **ØMQ** and **RabbitMQ** (both message queue services) may be of your interest in achieving this. They can act as proxies for your data storage servers, creating the idea that you have a big and unified storage server. These services are targeted to be performant and this is one of the use cases they're designed for.

Adding services to act like proxies adds another layer to your application environment. In small scenarios with a small dataset, they might be overkill. But in bigger datasets, even on a single storage server, they can help maintain a constant throughput while your dataset grows.

# Clustering data

Spreading services across different hosts will be necessary. Somewhere, while your application dataset is growing, you'll see your host screaming for resources and your average load gradually eating up every one of your processors. From that moment onward, you need to add a host to keep the speed stable and allow your dataset to grow a little more.

Moving from using one host to using two hosts can be complex, forcing you to dominate a database server or another type of data clustering. Many database services support clustering or some kind of replication. The following image is an example of a database replicated in the servers, allowing the application to access any of the database instances

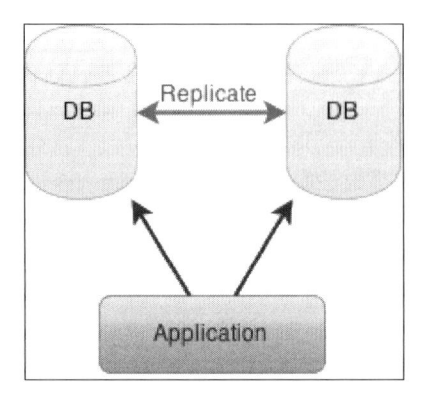

In multimaster replication mode, the dataset is usually stored (and duplicated) in two or more hosts, allowing the data to be updated from any of those hosts. This replicates data across all hosts, called **members**. Since there's no partitioning, every member is responsible for handling client requests.

These are some of the advantages:

- No single point of failure. Every member is a master, so everyone can fail.
- Hosts can be geographically distributed, allowing your application also to be distributed near your clients.

Some of the disadvantages are as follows:

- It's not usually consistent if in asynchronous mode, as the network may disappoint you before your data is replicated to another host
- It introduces latency if in some kind of synchronous mode, since your server won't reply to you until data is replicated, and once again your network may fail on you

There's no silver bullet, and for a really performant application, you definitely need to take a deep look into your data. You might need to split it between different types of servers, taking advantage of their unique features. As stated before, a message queue server might be the best choice for part of your data.

Replication does not allow you to scale properly. Your data is complete on every server. For huge datasets, this is a waste of space, given that the probability of all but one server going down is really small. And you have backups, right?

> There are better alternatives, such as clustering, where your data is partitioned and every block is replicated on at least two hosts. It's normally up to you to decide. This is similar to RAID5 on disks but without the *write hole* phenomenon (http://www.raid-recovery-guide.com/raid5-write-hole.aspx).

# Accessing data

Your application needs to be prepared for these scenarios. One of the possibilities is shown in the previous diagram. Your application knows about replication members and tries to use them randomly or by a specific rule. It's up to your application or database module to identify failures and handle them correctly. The following image describes how you can also replicate the application instances and introduce a proxy to intermediate access to the application.

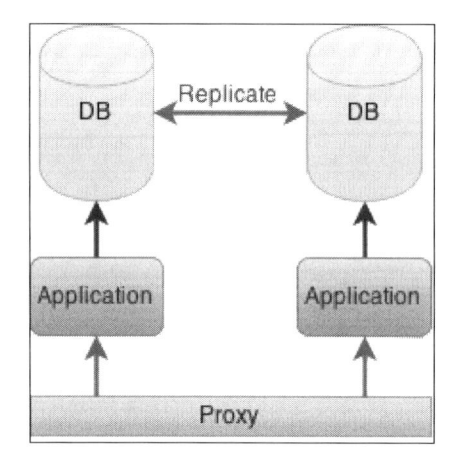

Another possible scenario is to have an instance of your application tied to each of your replication hosts, possibly even localhost. In this way, your application works locally. This, however, brings forth two issues to solve:

- Having a reverse proxy enables this to assign an application instance to each user depending on the user geographic location or application instance load.
- Your application needs to be able to work in this scenario (stateless), unless your proxy ensures that every client will always access the same instance

If your application only needs data stored in a database, these are the possible scenarios. If it depends on a filesystem, some scenarios won't fit unless you have some kind of synchronization between hosts. GlusterFS comes to my mind. If you don't need a filesystem and you're comfortable with some kind of object/blob storage, Ceph or even MongoDB can be a good choice. If you want a highly scalable data storage server, you might just start looking at Cassandra and forget about the alternatives. Prepare your application from the ground up to work with it and you won't regret it.

# Summary

Data is a critical part of your application and planning how to structure it is important. Even more important is how you plan your application growth and data escalation. Don't forget about caching for the most used parts of your data, and most importantly, don't forget backups. Replication and clustering are not kinds of backup. You need a correct backup plan that avoids downtime in the future. Don't forget to value your data.

In the next chapter, we'll continue with topics on application performance by seeing how and why tests are important and how you should benchmark and carefully read the results (with a grain of salt). Your application is almost ready for high performance. But before you go for production, make sure you test it thoroughly.

# 6
# Test, Benchmark, and Analyze

Testing your application is as important as its development. Testing is the process of analyzing your application modules and the application as a whole to see whether it behaves as you expect it. It allows your business to define use cases and check whether they're all accomplished.

There are many testing techniques. One of the most famous is **Test-driven Development** (**TDD**). This technique consists of using the smallest development cycles possible. Between every cycle, tests are performed and new tests and uses cases are added before they're developed. This way, your application versions can be continuously tested and any faulty version can be quickly spotted. If you use a version control system, such as Git, it becomes very easy to find the culprit of the failing test and fix it.

An important aspect of performing tests from the ground up is that you can keep adding use cases and test cases as you spot them. For example, if someone reports a bug and you create a specific use case for it, you can ensure that that bug doesn't appear again or that it will not be visible in the tests. In community-driven projects, it's very common to see this use case (a member spotting a bug and adding a test case for it). If you can replicate it, you can create a test case.

Depending on your test platform, you can benchmark your application. Usually, test platforms have a default timeout per test as long as 1 or 2 seconds. You can reduce this value for features that you want to ensure perform well. You can also do the opposite by giving more time for longer use cases.

Platforms with this timeout feature allow you to have consistent tests. Remember to test in a common platform, such as a general working environment. Don't define test benchmarks for a superfast server and then expect them to pass in a computer that is 20 years old.

# Test fundamentals

Tests can be defined in a variety of ways. The most common approach is unit testing. This is a method by which parts of your application are individually checked to confirm that they comply with the specifications. This approach encourages your application parts to act as independent and replaceable black boxes.

You need real data to properly test your application. You also need unrealistic data. Both are crucial to confirm that it behaves as expected with both correct data and scrambled data. This ensures that a misguided or malicious user won't break your application.

You might be wondering what I mean by unrealistic data. Does your application handle text in date fields or numbers in checkboxes? What about missing data? You might think it does, but if you have more developers working on it, you may want to ensure that, somewhere in the future, it doesn't stop behaving correctly. The most common type of bug occurs in one place after making a change in a completely different place.

The goal of unit testing should be to completely isolate each of your application's modules and to be able to test them independently. If a module needs other parts of the application to work properly, you can fake that data or mock that dependency, using Sinon (http://sinonjs.org/) for example.

Some of the benefits of testing are as follows:

- Bugs are found early in the development cycle. Since you can test your code every time you change it, bugs should be spotted earlier. The cost of fixing bugs earlier, sometimes even before going into production, greatly reduces overall costs.
- It forces developers to think about I/O data and errors, since application architects must think and properly describe every use case. Features and use cases are developed with one or more test cases in mind.
- It enables changing or refactoring modules while still ensuring that the expected behavior is kept intact because of the test cases.
- It facilitates module integration tests, since each of the modules are tested and have an expected behavior.

All of these benefits are achieved only if the tests are properly defined and your test covers the entire application (all functions and objects). With proper test coverage, you can also add specific use cases for new features or edge cases.

Separating tests for each module is quite difficult. For example, if one of your modules needs a database to work, your test case will require giving it database access. This is not good, since your unit test will actually be an integration test, and if it fails you won't be able to say whether the problem is with the module or with the database.

## The test environment

It is also important to have a consistent test environment. More importantly, the environment should be the same or almost the same, as the production environment. This means the same application (of course), but also the same operating system version, the same database server version, and so on.

For example, for Node.js tests, ensure that your test environment has the same Node.js version. You can test with different versions, but the most important is the version used in production. The same applies to the operative system version, the database service version, dependencies' versions, and so on.

## The Docker tool

Having the same environment might not be easy, but there's a solution for that—Linux containers. If you haven't tried Docker yet, you're missing the train. This solution is free and is a tool involving containers that makes them usable.

Its main difference compared to tools such as Vagrant is that it doesn't need a virtual machine to create an environment. Docker is similar to OpenVZ (`https://openvz.org/Main_Page`), but with a twist; you can create an environment (a container) and share it for others to use. If you like NPM, you will find this similar. You have versioning and dependencies, and the most used environments are already online for you to download and use.

You can create a test environment in a container and then distribute the container to other developers. This also applies to production. Your developers can get a snapshot of a production database and a complete production environment in their laptop. In this way, changes can be made and tested as if they were applied to production. This is better than trying in production and having to roll back. In this way, you'll roll back less often. This is the principle of continuous integration.

Let's create a very simple environment for our Node.js application. Have Docker installed, open a terminal, and run this code:

```
$ docker pull node:0.12.4
Pulling repository node
4797dc6f7a9c: Download complete
...
6abd33745acb: Download complete
Status: Downloaded newer image for node:0.12.4
```

Remember that we want a specific version, and that's why we're forcing 0.12.4 in this case. I'm considering the operative system as unimportant, since our application won't have external dependencies or node modules. This command will just download the image template, and it's not creating any environment yet; we'll do that in a moment. You'll notice that it takes a few hundred megabytes. Don't worry; that is possibly the only space you need, as your environments will almost always depend on this image. If you want to check out the downloaded image, run this:

```
$ docker images
REPOSITORY          TAG         IMAGE ID            CREATED             VIRTUAL SIZE
node                0           4797dc6f7a9c        3 days ago          711.8 MB
node                0.12        4797dc6f7a9c        3 days ago          711.8 MB
node                latest      4797dc6f7a9c        3 days ago          711.8 MB
node                0.12.4      4797dc6f7a9c        3 days ago          711.8 MB
```

Well, there's a lot of space there, isn't there? If you look closely, you'll notice that there's only one image (the IMAGE ID is the same). What has happened is that 0.12.4 is actually the latest version by the time of writing this book, and the latest tag has also been assigned to our image. Furthermore, that version is the last version of 0.12, and it's the last version of 0.

This means that we can use any of these tags to refer to our image, but we don't want that, as new versions might come up and our images would start being built with those new versions.

We can see which containers are running, or were created before, and are not running anymore. We can see simply what is running, but I find it much more useful to see dead containers, as they potentially use unnecessary space. There are no containers now. We can simply test the image to see whether it works:

```
$ docker run -it node:0.12.4 bash
root@daa77af1b150:/# node -v
v0.12.4
root@daa77af1b150:/# npm -v
2.11.1
root@daa77af1b150:/# exit
```

We just ran a basic environment using our image, running `bash` in a `tty` (`-t`), in interactive mode (`-i`) as opposed to running in the background (`-d`). You can see that we have node and `npm` in the environment. If we look at which containers exist, we will see something similar to this:

```
$ docker ps -a
CONTAINER ID       IMAGE       COMMAND      CREATED ...
1a56bbeb3d36       node:0      "bash"       47 seconds ago ...
```

Our container has unique identifier, `1a56bbeb3d36`, is using the 0 node image, and is running the `bash` command. Well, it is actually no longer running. You can remove it by running this line:

```
$ docker rm 1a56bbeb3d36
```

Noticed the `Exited (0)` .. lines in the `ps` command? Yes, exit code from the command is accessible. If you exited `bash` with `exit 123`, you will see it outside the container. This is great for launching a test command instead of `bash` and then just checking whether all the tests have passed based on the exit code. You can also record the output and, in the event of a failure, save it for analysis.

## The test tool

Now that we have a form of replicating the environment to test, we need a proper test tool — something you can use to define your use cases and test cases. There are many great tools and Node.js has specific tools for testing. Some of them are really great.

If you have nothing in mind, I would recommend trying mocha (http://mochajs.org/). It's available for installation on NPM, and you should install it globally:

```
sudo npm install -g mocha
```

In this way, you can use mocha in all your applications on your computer without having to install it over and over again, because it's actually a development/test dependency, not a real application dependency. Installing it globally will also install the `mocha` command in your path.

Let's create a very simple module called `module.js` with a function that simply adds two numbers:

```
// add a with b
exports.add = function (a, b) {
  return a + b;
};
```

## Test, Benchmark, and Analyze

Now, let's create a test case. For this, we'll create another file called `test.js`:

```
var assert = require("assert");
var m      = require("./module");

describe("module.add()", function () {
  it("should add two numbers", function () {
    assert.equal(m.add(2, 3), 5);
  });
});
```

As you can see, this file loads our module (m) and asserts that `m.add` should add two numbers. To check it, we add a test case by checking whether the module returns 5 when we pass 2 and 3 to it. Now, open a terminal in the folder where you have these two files and just run `mocha` without any arguments, like this:

```
~/test > ls -l
total 16
-rw-r--r--  1 dresende  staff   66 Jun 14 17:08 module.js
-rw-r--r--  1 dresende  staff  191 Jun 14 17:08 test.js
~/test > mocha


  module.add()
    ✓ should add two numbers


  1 passing (9ms)

~/test >
```

Nice, isn't it? There are other forms of output called **reporters**, such as the progress, list, or dot matrix. If you just want a simple output, try list or progress. If you want the details of every test, use the spec reporter. It's shown in the preceding screenshot.

Let's add another test to our function. Change the test file to look like this:

```
var assert = require("assert");
var m      = require("./module");

describe("module.add()", function () {
  it("should add two numbers", function () {
    assert.equal(m.add(2, 3), 5);
  });

  it("should return null when one is not a number", function () {
    assert.equal(m.add(2, "a"), null);
  });
});
```

If you run mocha again, your test case will cause the `test` suite to fail, as shown in this screenshot:

```
~/test > mocha

  module.add()
    ✓ should add two numbers
    1) should return null when one is not a number


  1 passing (16ms)
  1 failing

  1) module.add() should return null when one is not a number:
     AssertionError: '2a' == null
      at Context.<anonymous> (test.js:10:10)
```

Let's change our module to behave correctly, as we stated in our new test. You can change it however you want; I'll just show an example:

```
// add a with b
exports.add = function (a, b) {
  if (isNaN(a) || isNaN(b)) {
    return null;
  }
  return a + b;
};
```

Upon running again, our test should pass, as shown in the following screenshot:

```
~/test > mocha

  module.add()
    ✓ should add two numbers
    ✓ should return null when one is not a number


  2 passing (10ms)

~/test >
```

We can now test this in our environment instead of testing it directly. This ensures that our application works in a clean environment and is not passing because of something your local environment has. To do this, we can use our previous node image. Let's create a simple test environment. To do this, we need to create a file called `Dockerfile` in our test folder:

```
FROM node:0.12.4

RUN npm install -g mocha

VOLUME /opt/app/
```

This describes our environment. What the file is describing is as follows:

- Use node image version `0.12.4`
- Install the `mocha` dependency
- Create a linkable volume on `/opt/app`

Now, let's build our environment and call it `env/test`. We're actually creating a new image based on another image. Our linkable volume is a folder that we can specify when running our environment. In this way, you can use this very image for all your applications. To build our environment, we run this:

```
$ Sending build context to Docker daemon 11.26 kB
Sending build context to Docker daemon
Step 0 : FROM node:0.12.4
 ---> 4797dc6f7a9c
Step 1 : RUN npm install -g mocha
 ---> Running in 286c8bb64a2b
...
Removing intermediate container 26fd9bb79ed5
Successfully built e36af32c961c
```

We now have an image that we can use. Let's try the image by running our tests with `mocha`.

```
~/test > docker run -it --rm -v `pwd`:/opt/app env/test mocha /opt/app

  module.add()
    ✓ should add two numbers
    ✓ should return null when one is not a number


  2 passing (11ms)

~/test >
```

Check out the online documentation of Docker for details on the command line. We're running our image where the `/opt/app` (`-v`) volume is our current folder (with our Node.js files). Our test environment is run in interactive mode (`-it`), and the result image is discarded at the end (`--rm`).

If you have a central code repository, it is good practice to test before committing to avoid common mistakes. It also avoids breaking changes. It's common to make a change to fix or improve something and break something else. With an always-clean test environment, developers can ensure that the tests run correctly. This environment can be similar to the one in the following image:

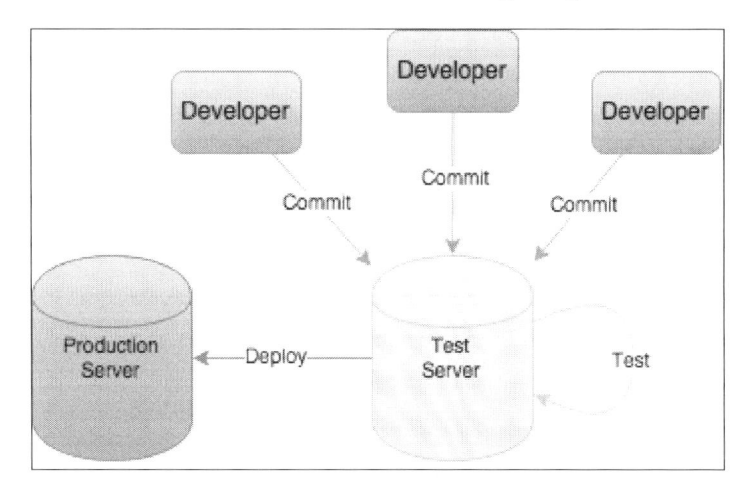

# Continuous integration

**Continuous integration** (**CI**) is a practice wherein all the developers of an application continuously integrate their changes into a central repository. This is a practice used in **extreme programming** (**XP**). It introduces new features faster and helps avoid code conflicts by reducing code merge time.

If the application has a good test suite, developers can test changes locally in a replicated production and test environments and just commit if they pass. These tests should not replace the tests done on the server. If the test suite executes fast, it could even be a guarantee for the commit to be merged, but this is usually not recommended, as some commits actually cannot pass. Usually, all the commits are accepted and only then are they tested. The test results should be public at least inside the developer's circle as a way of forcing them to take care of their commits, how they structure their code, and how they describe commits.

There are four best practices for CI:

- Have a code repository and use a revision control system
- Every commit should be checked to guarantee that it passes all the tests
- Separate the test environment from production environment
- Automate deployment

One way of achieving this workflow is by using **git**. Since it allows you to define hooks for commits and merges, you can add a hook to the central repository to test every new commit. If the commit passes, it could be eligible to pass to production.

One strategy can be to merge the latest commit that passed all the tests with production. This could be every time a commit passes or at specific times. For simple applications, this approach is acceptable. But if you have a big user base, it can really be risky. Ensure that your test base is really good, and at least look and read the commit change log. There are risks that you should know of, as follows:

- Your test base might not cover all of your code. This means that there are parts of your code that are not tested, which raises uncertainty about its behavior. In this case, you should try to cover as much of your code as possible.
- Your test base might not cover all of your use cases. If all of your use cases are not described in the tests, they will not be tested in your code. They could get handled correctly, but it's still uncertain. So, you should describe all of your use cases.

- There are test cases which aren't easy to describe or even reproduce. You should make an effort to avoid these kinds of tests and ensure that you can completely rely on tests. Otherwise, you'll need someone to test the application changes before they go to production.

Also, it is important to be able to test the application against your production database, perhaps the latest backup or a database with replication that you can use without compromising the production environment.

Data size always influences your application's performance. If you're just testing your modules to check simple use cases, you're not testing the load, but you should. Sometimes, your production data can have relationships that you didn't except at first. You may think your code doesn't allow those relationships to appear, but you may be wrong.

Consider, for example, a hierarchical structure in which you define a parent for a certain element. Assume that this descendant can also be a parent of another element. What if a third-degree descendant is a parent of an ascendant? This creates a loop that you probably don't want but you have to handle. Even if your application doesn't allow this loop to appear at first, consider getting the code required to protect yourself against it.

## Code coverage

Having all of your code covered by tests is important to ensure that you're really testing everything, or at least everything that is coded. This is not an easy task. Conditions and loops in your code create a log of different cases and running paths, and some of your code might be triggered only in very specific situations. That situation needs to be tested somehow.

Code coverage is a metric used to indicate how much of your code is covered by your test suite. A higher metric indicates that your application is more "test covered" and can usually be an indication of low bug probability. This metric is usually given in percentage values, and 50 percent coverage means that half of your code covered by the test suite.

There are tools that can help you find this value, otherwise it would be impossible to calculate it. In a Node.js environment, what the tools usually do is creating a replica of your code, in which they change every significant line to get a way of counting the number of times the execution passed through that line. Significant lines are lines with real code, not comments or empty lines.

There are also online services for doing this. Depending on your application license or budget, you might prefer to prepare your test environment locally. This is usually not as simple as it might look. You have to create a way of instrumenting your code (this is best done on a copy) and running your tests while gathering the coverage metrics, and then generate a report.

There are several tools for Node.js that you can try. There's no magic tool, and you should see what fits you and your application best. One possible tool is `istanbul`. Let's try it out on our small test example. You'll see that it's a little tricky, and for a real application, you must automate this process. Let's start by installing the dependencies:

```
sudo npm install -g istanbul mocha-istanbul
```

The `mocha-istanbul` dependency can be installed locally. The `istanbul` Node.js module should be global because it has a command for us to use. Now we can instrument our code. Let's create an instrumented copy:

```
istanbul instrument module.js > instrumented.js
```

We now have to change our test suite to use our instrumented version:

```
var assert = require("assert");
var m      = require("./instrumented");

describe("module.add()", function () {
  it("should add two numbers", function () {
    assert.equal(m.add(2, 3), 5);
  });

  it("should return null when one is not a number", function () {
    assert.equal(m.add(2, "a"), null);
  });
});
```

Finally, we just need to run our test suite using the `istanbul` reporter. To do this, run `mocha` with the `reporter` parameter:

```
mocha -reporter mocha-istanbul test.js
```

Instead of showing a description of the tests, you'll see a report showing how many lines and functions are instrumented in your code and covered by the test suite. Here's an example of the output:

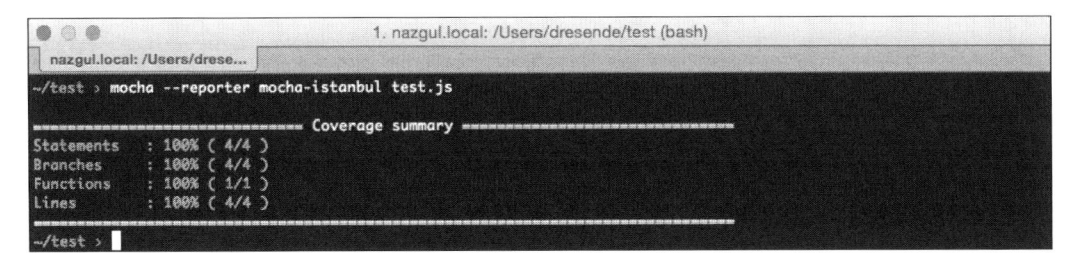

```
~/test > mocha --reporter mocha-istanbul test.js
============================ Coverage summary ============================
Statements   : 100% ( 4/4 )
Branches     : 100% ( 4/4 )
Functions    : 100% ( 1/1 )
Lines        : 100% ( 4/4 )
==========================================================================
~/test >
```

After this, you should have a folder called `html-report` with an `index.html` page inside. Open it in your browser to analyze your test coverage. You should see a page similar to the following screenshot:

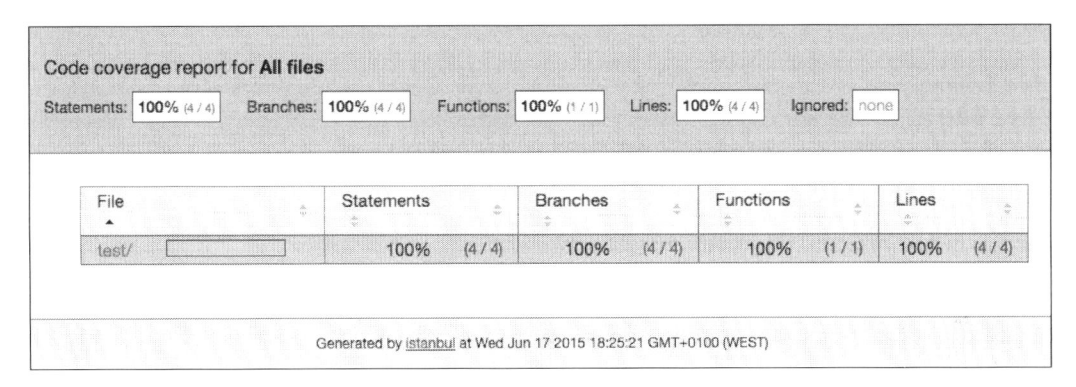

**Code coverage report for All files**

Statements: 100% (4/4)  Branches: 100% (4/4)  Functions: 100% (1/1)  Lines: 100% (4/4)  Ignored: none

| File | Statements | Branches | Functions | Lines |
|---|---|---|---|---|
| test/ | 100% (4/4) | 100% (4/4) | 100% (1/1) | 100% (4/4) |

Generated by istanbul at Wed Jun 17 2015 18:25:21 GMT+0100 (WEST)

You'll see the `test` folder, and inside, you'll find our original module. Click on it and you'll see a coverage report. For each significant line (notice that the lines with closing brackets are ignored), you'll have a number associated. It corresponds to the number of times the execution passed that line while we we're testing. In our case, it's the **1** and **2** columns with a green background. It's easy to understand why, seeing that we have only two tests.

## Benchmark tests

Benchmarking is the process of running a set of tools or tests to measure specific performance metrics in order to compare them, either with other tools or with past tests. The most common benchmark tests for applications are related to two similar metrics: time (of an operation) and operations (over a period of time).

To maintain your application's performance, you need to continuously benchmark it. One obvious approach is to use the test suite, where you add specific tests just for benchmarking purposes. After checking out the common use cases, you can have specific tests where you can ensure that certain operations continue to run for a specific target time.

Take benchmarking seriously, but don't lose sleep over it! Most of the time, when you start your application development, you just don't have the statistics to compare with and you don't know what benchmark tests to define.

Start by benchmarking simple listings, such as history lists, and ensure that they don't perform over the 100-millisecond mark. When creating a more complex interface, ensure that its rendering also performs well. People tend to stress out if they have to wait for more than half a second for a simple task, and more than one or two seconds for a more complex one.

These benchmarks are usually done using a copy of the production data, or a subset of it if it's too large, in order to ensure that you're benchmarking against a good amount of data and not a small set of data on a test environment like your personal laptop. You can also perform the test against the production data, but I won't recommend it.

For example, using our previous test framework, `mocha` ensures that each test runs for less than two seconds. You can change this default timeout for specific tests. Let's try it out with a new test file called `timeout.js`:

```
describe("timeout", function () {
  this.timeout(100); // milliseconds

  it("will fail", function (done) {
    // we should call done() but we don't to cause timeout
  });
});
```

We're creating an asynchronous test. This is because we referenced `done` in our test function to be called when the test ends. In this case, we're not calling it specifically to force it to fail. Let's try it, as follows:

It is good practice to use timeouts in specific tests where performance is important. The normal timeout may be fine for most common tests, but make sure that you analyze some specific tests and ensure that they perform within a certain period of time.

That timeout can be a performance limit or just a mark to inform you when your application is becoming too complex or when your test data is becoming too big to be able to keep up that performance. That's when, based on the previous chapter, you need to take a look at your environment and analyze your next steps.

Test suites such as mocha can also give you other interesting information that complements your tests and helps you get a better picture of the behavior of your application, such as:

- Report test durations, even for the tests that are not benchmark tests, this will allow you to first make your tests and look at the metrics, and then define a good timeout mark.
- Present test reports. They can be used for quality assurance reports and can be saved for later analysis or comparison.

Specifically for Node.js applications, `mocha` can provide you with:

- Memory leak detection, by looking at global variables before and after the tests
- Uncaught exception detection, indicating the test that caused it
- Seamless asynchronous support
- Node.js debugger support
- Browser support

## Analyzing tests

Having a test suite is very important. The most important benefit is having your application fully tested, or at least as much tested as possible. Creating the initial test environment may be a challenge, but it pays off as you keep developing your application.

Performing proper tests ensures that you:

- Don't reintroduce old bugs with new features. This can happen even without touching the source code and just by making a database change.
- Can define use cases by defining test cases first (look at `https://en.wikipedia.org/wiki/Test-driven_development`).
- Can make changes and easily check whether the application keeps behaving as expected.
- Can check your test coverage and see how it has changed over time.
- Can create specific tests for newly found bugs and ensure that they don't reappear.
- Ensure that benchmark tests run under a specific metric.

Getting a proper test suite is similar to having a quality assurance person test your application every time you make a change. Moreover, your quality assurance person won't be as precise or as fast as your test suite.

If your application has more developers than just you, make sure that you enforce tests passing successfull and a test coverage of a high mark like 90 percent. If you automate your coverage tests, you can use the coverage metric as a condition to merge new features with production.

Make sure that your tests are public in the development group circle, allowing everyone to see the work of others. This motivates people to work better, as their reputation is public, at least inside the group.

When there are more people looking at tests, developers can share experiences and ask for help upon bumping into failing tests. This reduces the time taken to fix a problem and motivates developers to keep the test suite always going. It should be a constant goal—to keep the test history clean of failures.

# Summary

A good, performant application is all about how well it performs. A complete test suite ensures that you also perform well in developing and can introduce changes fast—changes that can improve performance. The test suite should have specific tests for benchmark analysis, with demanding time restrictions. The developers should know about them and work hard to keep the tests passing without having to lift those restrictions.

Use the test suite as a metric for production. Ensure that you merge new changes if your test suite covers your application source in at least 90 percent coverage and passes all the benchmark tests. Use a separate server for those tests, and don't mix tests with production. Keep your production server lean and fast, and change it only if you're sure it will keep that way.

In the next chapter, we'll look at bottlenecks—limits that degrade performance—and the situations in which you can't do anything about them. You must try hard to be ready for them and, if possible, try to attenuate their consequences. The network, the server, and the client are some of the factors that introduce bottlenecks. Some you can control and minimize, but others… you just have to be ready for them.

# 7
# Bottlenecks

As we've seen in the previous chapters, a lot of elements influence performance. Even the process of development will influence how you monitor performance degradation. The patterns you use might not make a difference on a small scale, but after deployment, you'll regret every bad decision you made.

The host is also an important performance factor. How well your processor performs for your specific tasks is important. How much memory you have available influences how much of your data will reside in a fast location or will move to a slower location, such as a local disk.

Caching your data is also of great importance. The technique of accelerating data access using some kind of middle storage to give a perception of greater speed creates an important illusion of a fast application. Although this might seem wrong since it looks like an illusion, it's actually very important if you want to stretch performance to the limit.

All of this is important, but there are limits that you cannot pass, or at least some that you should know in order to go around and choose a better design pattern. Some of these limits are outside your scope and you cannot tweak or control them. Others could be minimized if you have the budget and/or time and want to take that path. I recommend that you take it, as knowing the surroundings of your application will give you a bigger picture of the understanding of how it all works and how it could be improved.

# Host limits

The place where you host your application—the server—has limits. There are two types of limits on the host: hardware and software. Hardware limits can be easy to spot. Your application might be consuming all of the memory and needing to consume disk to continue working. Adding more memory by upgrading your host, whether physical or virtual, seems to be the right choice.

For Node.js applications you also have a software memory limit imposed by V8, so don't forget about this when upgrading your memory banks. As a 32-bit environment has a limit of more or less 3.5 GB, I'm assuming that you're upgrading memory in a 64-bit environment. In this case, your application would be running by default at a 1 GB V8 limit. You then need to run your application with a higher limit by starting it in a way similar to the following command:

```
$ node --max_old_space_size 4000 application
```

This would run `application.js` with a 4 GB memory limit. This is actually not recommended. You have probably chosen a design pattern that is not suitable for the task, and you should try to split your application into smaller services.

When you don't control your production environment other restrictions might apply, such as the inability to install a software dependency or upgrade a library to fix a security or performance issue. If you don't control the environment from top to bottom, you're not stretching its limits.

Operating systems and database servers usually come with predefined values for moderated usage. This is usually fine for the average user, but definitely not enough for the power user.

A simple example is the maximum number of open file descriptors for each process. A socket is a file descriptor, and if you use the default 1024 limit it means that at most you'll probably have 1,000 open clients connected. I'm being generous; I'm talking about a Linux machine. If you look at OS X, you will have a worse scenario.

Similar to this limit, and looking at Linux in particular, you can check out the other limits that definitely influence your application. Look at the manual and see what options you might want to tweak. The following is an example of the limits and defaults you may find in a Linux system:

```
$ ulimit -a
core file size          (blocks, -c) 0
data seg size           (kbytes, -d) unlimited
scheduling priority             (-e) 0
file size               (blocks, -f) unlimited
```

```
pending signals                     (-i) 31692
max locked memory       (kbytes, -l) 64
max memory size         (kbytes, -m) unlimited
open files                          (-n) 1024
pipe size               (512 bytes, -p) 8
POSIX message queues      (bytes, -q) 819200
real-time priority                  (-r) 0
stack size              (kbytes, -s) 8192
cpu time                (seconds, -t) unlimited
max user processes                  (-u) 31692
virtual memory          (kbytes, -v) unlimited
file locks                          (-x) unlimited
```

There are other methods and options that you can change and optimize for your application. I'm talking about kernel parameters. You can look at them and change them using the `sysctl` command.

You can tweak areas such as the filesystem, network timings and routing, the virtual memory behavior, and the kernel itself, like processor scheduling and reaction to hanging tasks.

Here's a small list showing just a fraction of the options:

```
$ sysctl -a | tail
vm.overcommit_ratio = 50
vm.page-cluster = 3
vm.panic_on_oom = 0
vm.percpu_pagelist_fraction = 0
vm.scan_unevictable_pages = 0
vm.stat_interval = 1
vm.swappiness = 60
vm.user_reserve_kbytes = 131072
vm.vfs_cache_pressure = 100
vm.zone_reclaim_mode = 0
```

As mentioned before, it's not just the operating system that can be badly optimized for your use case. Services usually come with a simple default configuration that is not targeted at performance.

MySQL database servers can have some weird configuration parameters, such as `innodb_flush_log_at_trx_commit`, which defaults to 1. This means that every transaction triggers a flush to disk (to save the transaction). If you have 100 transactions per second, it means your disk will heat and degrade performance by issuing 100 flushes per second.

Instead, you would want to ensure that this configuration is 2, which means that disk flush is done at most once per second. This configuration does not ensure ACID (https://en.wikipedia.org/wiki/ACID) compliance, but I think you'll thank me later. Performance comes at a cost, and in this case, an uninterruptible power supply is required.

Another configuration you must watch out for is the memory used by the operative system and all the services involved in your application. For instance, taking the MySQL server, you must ensure that it doesn't consume all of the memory and leaves some for your other services. This avoids swaps and ensures that it runs smoothly.

## Network limits

The network is nowadays the de facto transport method for accessing applications. As the Internet of Things becomes more of a reality, even common desktop applications, such as office productivity tools, are moving to the cloud. You probably didn't ever develop a traditional desktop application.

Cloud applications give you many advantages over traditional ones, such as the following:

- Easier deployments. Since the application is located in one or more central points, it's simpler to fix a bug or add a feature to all of your user base.
- License enforcements. As the application is not installed in the user's computer and you control the host, you can block its usage or control the quality of service.
- Proper environment. Because you control the host, you ensure that it has a proper processor and enough memory and disk space to operate as it should.

All of these are very good pros, but what about the cons? Well, for every advantage, there's usually a disadvantage. It's not good or bad; it just depends on what you prefer. Taking the previous list, we can enumerate the counterparts:

- Deployments must be made with care, as a server contains sensitive data and it is the only way to use your application. Do you accept Gmail being offline for 15 minutes? To guarantee a proper deployment, you need proper infrastructure with data duplicated to ensure that you can remove servers from the network pool, update them, and redeploy them again.
- Enforcing a license means that you keep a service online and no downtime is accepted. Similarly, you may need to ensure a billing system while the user is using the application. This is the opposite of a common desktop application, where you pay once and then forget about it.

- Adapting application to multiple environments. Supporting all major browser vendors is not easy. With this comes the user's assumption that your application must have a mobile-friendly alternative, which usually doesn't exist in a desktop version.

There are a lot of market offers (free and paid) to "convert" your web application into a desktop application if you prefer the advantages of not moving your application to the cloud.

Applications now prefer to reside in the cloud. Their advantages usually surpass those of desktop applications, and there's something important mentioned in the advantages—licensing. The cloud gives you the "as a service" opportunity, which you usually don't have in a traditional application.

With the cloud come a lot of hard work and troubles. You need to register your own domain, pay for a dedicated or shared host, and deploy your application. If you're developing a big application and want to live up to your promises, you need more than that: hardware, a network link with a good quality of service, a support team, a backup plan, and so on.

No matter what you choose, there are limits you should be aware of. You probably know them but this is never reflected. You have limits such as these:

- Responsiveness. When the user interacts using the application interface, it might feel slow, as the interface is being downloaded from the cloud as the user is using the interface. This responsiveness can be improved if you cache the interface in the user's computer. Caching means that sometimes the user might be looking at an old interface, but that might not be as critical as getting a fast user experience. There are standards for doing this. Take a look at the Offline Web Applications section of the HTML standard as an example.

- Data access, when a user interacts with a more data-intensive interface. Sometimes, part of the slowness of the interface is related to your server collecting data from the database and sending it through the network. You can also use a cache, but you may have to be more careful because interface caching is one thing and data caching is another. People can tolerate one or two hours with an old interface, but not with old data.

> Security is critical. Offer HTTPS access to your users so that they can feel comfortable about their privacy.

Apart from these limits, there are security issues that reduce performance. For example, in terms of privacy you have to choose HTTPS, which means a good certificate and good server configuration to avoid poor ciphers. This in turn means that some users might be unable to access the application, and data exchange between the server and the client will be a bit slower.

This is a requirement if you want to ensure that the data being transferred from the server to the end user is not compromised. However, this is actually not enough because the user must also have an up-to-date browser and a good configuration. There have been a lot of SSL weaknesses found recently, and they can be avoided by updating the browser.

Networking was not designed to be secure; it was designed with the assumption that everyone has good intentions, which is definitely wrong. When your users access your application using a public hotspot (from a coffee shop, a mall, or an airport), they're vulnerable to privacy issues. Attackers can sniff the network traffic and try to find a password or attach themselves to an open session and be able to impersonate a user.

Getting a secure connection is important, but it might reduce performance and also the number of users that each of your servers can handle. This can be the cost of security. Think that HTTPS is always slower? Try `http://www.httpvshttps.com/`.

Also, don't forget about your database. Ensure that you don't have any default password and you only allow access from your application (don't give access to everyone on the Internet).

Security does not end here. As your application is a known network location, you can be the victim of an attack. Perhaps you think that putting the server behind a firewall and just redirecting traffic to the ports that the users need (such as HTTP and HTTPS) is enough, but don't forget **Denial of Service** (**DoS**) attacks. An attacker with an attack network can bring your application down by just forcing it to be so busy with them that real users won't be able to access and use it. This gives them a perception of poor performance and is something you can't avoid.

For example, GitHub faced an attack from China in March 2015. It lasted a few days. They couldn't avoid it and could only mitigate it by trying to deflect the traffic. Some people were greatly affected. As your application becomes bigger, more attackers may be interested in your information or just in denying access to it.

# Client limits

Clients also have limits. They may be using an operating system that you don't know or can't be sure about. This also applies to the browser, the applications installed, and even the location.

> Never trust the user agent sent by browsers. Also, don't ever infer any information from it. It can be forged to be anything. A laptop can mimic a Nokia phone from the last century very easily — no hacking is necessary!

This is something every developer must observe as a rule: never trust the client. I'm not saying this in a bad way, but you have to be sure of the information you have. For example, your interface has validations in forms and you're sure that they validate correctly before submitting, right? Wrong! Never trust the client.

Also, never trust the link between the client and you. Validate information again on the server side. If possible, by using Node.js, use the same code to validate on both sides and avoid duplicated code. For example, you can use some code to validate a form in a web view and that code can also be used in the server. Don't forget! Node.js is JavaScript. If it's a complex piece of code or module, you may want to look at browserify (`http://browserify.org/`).

Form validations should be done on both sides to give a perception of performance and to actually avoid common errors. You shouldn't validate everything on the client, but at least check whether a currency field actually has a number and not text, and confirm that all the required fields have proper values. This reduces the round trips of submitting to the server and the server replying back with an error.

Apart from the limits of the application, there are limits outside that you can't control. The user will always blame you, and perhaps it's not your application's fault most of the time. Are you prepared for an intermittent connection for a client from a cellular network? I'm not referring to 3G, because this can be stable enough. I'm referring to GPRS connections.

Do you have a full-blown application for a cellphone that does not have a more than 300-pixel wide screen and behaves like my TI-83 from high school? Are you expecting that everyone will use the latest cellphone with a huge screen and more processor power than your netbook? It's here that the sense of performance is noticed.

A huge application can bring down a weaker cellphone just by rendering the interface. A cheap processor will have a hard time rendering all the elements and running all of the JavaScript in your application. It will be a challenge for it to render on a small screen. Therefore, it's better to have a completely different interface for this type of screen and simply use an adaptive interface for smaller differences.

The user accepts a different interface because they are actually interfacing with the application in a different way. They are probably using a finger on a cellphone and a mouse or a couple of fingers on a tablet or a laptop. Also, the distance between the eyes and the screen is different, hence the resolution difference.

Because of this and to target the best performance possible, you should bring forth a simpler interface. Remove clutter-like information that the user will probably not need, for example, in a cellphone. Keep only the important actions. If possible, cache the interface for a better sense of performance. It's better to see a spinning wheel than a blank screen with no progress information.

Nowadays, the Web gives you choices. You can use different types of devices with different systems and web browsers. This is good for the user but horrible for the developer. It's a fragmentation that forces applications to be developed with only a couple of targets in mind and not all of the market.

You need to focus on the main target of the application and develop the best interface for it. You can then move your focus to other environments, such as the smaller screens on cellphones and watches. Don't make an application that can run on all screens but isn't the best on any of them.

A few years ago, applications were copied to all screens, which was actually dumb. People use different devices with different goals in mind. For example, people won't want to create a task list on a cellphone, but will probably want to check it and mark it as complete. This means that you can have in place a much smaller application to do exactly what the user wants, avoiding excessive information and the risk of slowing down interaction and degrading experience.

## Browser limits

Browser vendors are merging efforts to make the lives of developers easier. A few years ago, it was hell to develop a web application for several browsers. You would usually focus on one or two of them. If you focused on more, your code would get a lot more complicated and performance would be compromised. Usually, applications would become slower with time and with newer browser versions.

Nowadays, it's safer to develop an application in only one browser. Most of the application, if not all—depending on what abstraction you used for the DOM (jQuery is the best example)—will run just fine on other browsers. You can then make a couple of improvements, and you will have an application running smoothly on every browser.

Keeping these abstraction layers up to date is important to avoid deprecated and slower code. Browsers tend to release versions more often and bring newer developer interfaces that those abstractions take advantage of.

**Test runner**

Done. Ready to run again.                                                    Run again

Testing in Chrome 43.0.2357.124 on OS X 10.10.3

| Test | | | Ops/sec |
|---|---|---|---|
| jQuery 1.3.2 | `tests($jq132);` | | 21,947 ±3.11% 77% slower |
| jQuery 1.4.x | `tests($jq14);` | | 28,068 ±2.51% 70% slower |
| jQuery 1.6.x | `tests($jq16);` | | 61,020 ±2.86% 35% slower |
| jQuery 1.8.3 | `tests($jq183);` | | 65,470 ±1.89% 30% slower |
| jQuery 1.9.1 | `tests($jq191);` | | 70,215 ±2.31% 25% slower |
| jQuery 1.10.1 | `tests($jq1101);` | | 91,629 ±2.85% fastest |
| jQuery 2.1.0 | `tests($jq210);` | | 94,035 ±3.02% fastest |
| JQuery 1.7.2 | `tests($jq172);` | | 61,212 ±1.94% 34% slower |

The preceding screenshot is a `jsperf` testing some versions of jQuery. The versions are not actually the latest ones, but it doesn't matter. Take it with a grain of salt. As you can see, the newer versions perform better—not always, but this is usually true. You can see how, in this example, the performance of the oldest version is 77 percent worse than the newest one.

## Performance variables

Performance should be seen as a mixture of choices and variables that you should adjust depending on your needs. Here are some variables you should consider:

- Choose the best or second best platform. Remember that the best one could potentially not be the best for you.
- Define your data structure and choose your database server wisely. Think big and plan how you'll react to fast data growth.
- Plan your application's modules and don't forget about making tests to every module. Create a developing environment that can be replicated in order for it to be easier for new developers to start programming faster.
- Choose a target environment and start developing. Don't start developing for every device and browser.

## Summary

Your application's performance is not constrained by your code and database choices. There are limitations that you must be aware of in order to choose the best path for your application. These are just external elements of your application that influence its performance, but there are others as well.

The most important rule—you shouldn't forget it—is to plan your steps. Don't develop without thinking properly about this. A bad choice will make your life harder later on when you have to fix it. It's better to lose an hour thinking than a week fixing. That's actually part of your own development performance.

# Index

## A

**ab tool**
  URL 5
**Active Record pattern** 18
**Adapter pattern** 23
**anti-patterns** 14
**application behavior**
  monitoring 3, 4
**architectural patterns**
  about 16
  Active Record pattern 18, 19
  Event-driven pattern 20
  Front Controller pattern 17
  Model-View-controller (MVC)
      pattern 17, 18
  Service Locator pattern 19, 20
**arrays** 31
**automatic memory management**
  about 35, 36
  event emitters 39
  heap snapshots 43-53
  memory leaks 38, 39
  memory organization 37, 38
  object heap 42, 43
  object representation 42
  referencing objects 40-42
  third-party management 54

## B

**behavioral patterns**
  about 25
  Mediator pattern 26
  Observer pattern 26
  Template method pattern 26

**ben tool**
  URL 5
**benchmarking** 2, 5
**benchmark tests**
  about 96-98
  load testing 5
  soak testing 6
  spike testing 6
**browserify**
  URL 107
**buffers** 29
**bugs, Node.js**
  buffer overflows 36
  dangling pointer bugs 36
  double free bugs 36
  memory leaks 36
**Builder pattern** 22

## C

**client limits** 107, 108
**Composite pattern** 24
**composition, in applications**
  about 6
  asynchronous tasks, embracing 8
  code, separating 7
  function rules, using 9, 10
  library functions, using 9
  modules, testing 10
  NPM, using 7
**continuous integration (CI)**
  about 92
  best practices 92
  code coverage 93-96
**creational patterns**
  about 21

Builder pattern  22
Factory method pattern  21
Lazy initialization pattern  21
Object pool pattern  23
Singleton pattern  22

## D

database management system (DBMS)
  about  73, 74
  asynchronous caching  75-77
  backups  73
  data, accessing  80
  data, caching  74
  data, clustering  78, 79
  management  73
  security  73
  structure  73
data storage
  about  72
  excessive I/O  72
Decorator pattern  24
Denial of Service (DoS)  106
docker tool  85-87
duplex stream  29

## E

ECMAScript  1
eval call  32
event-driven architecture
  about  27, 28
  buffers  29
  streams  28, 29
Event-driven pattern  20
event emitters  39
events  15
extreme programming (XP)  92

## F

Facade pattern  25
Factory method pattern  21
Fibonacci  57-61
fibonacci function  60
flame graph
  about  63-66
  URL  63

for-in loops  32
Front Controller pattern  17
functions
  about  31
  using  9, 10

## G

Garbage Collector (GC)  35
git  92

## H

heap snapshots  43-46
hidden types  30
high performance
  about  1
  obtaining  4
host limits
  about  102, 103
  browser limits  108, 109
  client limits  107, 108
  hardware  102
  network limits  104-106
  performance variables  110
httpload tool
  URL  5
HTTPS
  URL  106

## I

infinite loops  32
Inversion of Control  26
I/O library
  about  56, 57
  Fibonacci  57-61
  flame graph  62-68
  profiling, alternatives  68

## J

JSCS
  URL  9
JSON  72

## L

Lazy initialization pattern  21
lazy sweep  42
library functions
  using  9
libuv  56
load testing  5

## M

Mediator pattern  26
members  79
memorizing technique  60
memory leak  38, 39
Model-View-Adapter (MVA)  18
Model-View-controller (MVC)
        pattern  17, 18
Model-View-ViewModel (MVVM)  18

## N

network limits  104-106
Node.js
  about  1, 2
  patterns  15
  URL  10
Node.js Package Manager (NPM)
  about  6
  using  7
nonblocking API
  about  1
  buffers  1
  streams  1
numbers  30

## O

object heap  42, 43
Object pool pattern  23
object-relational mapping (ORM)  18
Observer pattern  26
old space  38
OpenVZ
  URL  85
optimizations
  about  29
  arrays  31
  eval call  32
  for-in loops  32
  functions  31
  hidden types  30
  infinite loops  32
  numbers  30
  try-catch blocks  32

## P

patterns
  about  13, 14
  architectural patterns  16
  behavioral patterns  25
  creational patterns  21
  structural patterns  23
  types  16
performance
  analysis  2, 3
  variables  110
planning  4
profiling
  about  2, 55
  alternatives  68
Proxy pattern  25

## R

RabbitMQ  78
RAID5
  URL  79
readable stream  28
reporters  88
Retained size  38

## S

Service Locator pattern  19, 20
service-oriented architecture (SOA)  27
Sessions  27
shallow size  37
Singleton pattern  22
Sinon
  URL  84
soak testing  6
spike testing  6

**streams**
  about  2, 15, 28
  duplex  29
  readable  28
  transform  29
  writable  29
**structural patterns**
  about  23
  Adapter pattern  23
  Composite pattern  24
  Decorator pattern  24
  Facade pattern  25
  Proxy pattern  25

# T

**Template method pattern  26**
**test**
  analyzing  98, 99
  benchmark tests  96-98
  benefits  84
  continuous integration (CI)  92
  docker tool  85-87
  environment  85
  fundamentals  84
  test tool  87-91

**Test-driven Development (TDD)  83**
**test tool  87-91**
**transform stream  29**
**trashed memory**
  identifying  40-42
**try-catch blocks  32**
**Twitter  6**

# U

**Unix pipes**
  URL  28

# V

**V8  3**
**V8 Tick Processor**
  URL  58

# W

**writeable stream  29**

# Thank you for buying
# Node.js High Performance

## About Packt Publishing

Packt, pronounced 'packed', published its first book, *Mastering phpMyAdmin for Effective MySQL Management*, in April 2004, and subsequently continued to specialize in publishing highly focused books on specific technologies and solutions.

Our books and publications share the experiences of your fellow IT professionals in adapting and customizing today's systems, applications, and frameworks. Our solution-based books give you the knowledge and power to customize the software and technologies you're using to get the job done. Packt books are more specific and less general than the IT books you have seen in the past. Our unique business model allows us to bring you more focused information, giving you more of what you need to know, and less of what you don't.

Packt is a modern yet unique publishing company that focuses on producing quality, cutting-edge books for communities of developers, administrators, and newbies alike. For more information, please visit our website at `www.packtpub.com`.

## About Packt Open Source

In 2010, Packt launched two new brands, Packt Open Source and Packt Enterprise, in order to continue its focus on specialization. This book is part of the Packt Open Source brand, home to books published on software built around open source licenses, and offering information to anybody from advanced developers to budding web designers. The Open Source brand also runs Packt's Open Source Royalty Scheme, by which Packt gives a royalty to each open source project about whose software a book is sold.

## Writing for Packt

We welcome all inquiries from people who are interested in authoring. Book proposals should be sent to `author@packtpub.com`. If your book idea is still at an early stage and you would like to discuss it first before writing a formal book proposal, then please contact us; one of our commissioning editors will get in touch with you.

We're not just looking for published authors; if you have strong technical skills but no writing experience, our experienced editors can help you develop a writing career, or simply get some additional reward for your expertise.

## Mastering Node.js

ISBN: 978-1-78216-632-0                Paperback: 346 pages

Expert techniques for building fast servers and scalable, real-time network applications with minimal effort

1. Master the latest techniques for building real-time, big data applications, integrating Facebook, Twitter, and other network services.

2. Tame asynchronous programming, the event loop, and parallel data processing.

3. Use the Express and Path frameworks to speed up development and deliver scalable, higher quality software more quickly.

## Instant Node.js Starter

ISBN: 978-1-78216-556-9                Paperback: 48 pages

Program your scalable network applications and web services with Node.js

1. Learn something new in an Instant! A short, fast, focused guide delivering immediate results.

2. Learn how to use module patterns and Node Packet Manager (NPM) in your applications.

3. Discover callback patterns in NodeJS.

Please check **www.PacktPub.com** for information on our titles

### Node Cookbook

ISBN: 978-1-84951-718-8    Paperback: 342 pages

Over 50 recipes to master the art of asynchronous server-side JavaScript using Node

1. Packed with practical recipes taking you from the basics to extending Node with your own modules.
2. Create your own web server to see Node's features in action.
3. Work with JSON, XML, web sockets, and make the most of asynchronous programming.

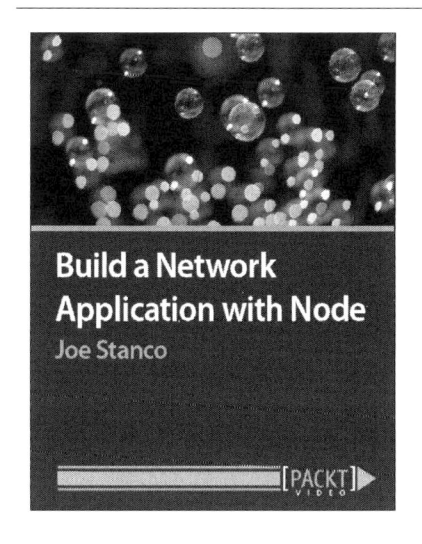

### Build a Network Application with Node [Video]

ISBN: 978-1-78216-827-0    Duration: 02:20 hours

Build, tune, and test a tangible Node.js application from start to finish

1. Offers the reader a primer in node conventions, along with best practices for publishing modules, optimizing performance, and organizing code.
2. Step-by-step examples that demonstrate how to progressively enhance your app.

Please check **www.PacktPub.com** for information on our titles

Printed in Great Britain
by Amazon.co.uk, Ltd.,
Marston Gate.